CATCHING
FIRE

...[John] spoke out and said to them all: "I baptize you with water; but there is one coming who is mightier than I am. I am not worthy to unfasten the straps of his sandals. He will baptize you with the Holy Spirit and with fire. His winnowing–shovel is ready in his hand, to clear his threshing–floor and gather the wheat into his granary; but the chaff he will burn on a fire that can never be put out." (Luke 3.16–17)

Abba Lot went to see Abba Joseph and said, "Abba, as much as I am able, I practise a small rule, all the little fasts, some prayer and meditation, and remain quiet; as much as possible I keep my thoughts clean. What else should I do?"

Then the old man stood up and stretched out his hands towards heaven, and his fingers became like the torches of flame. And he said, "Why not be turned into fire?" (Desert Fathers and Mothers)

As kingfishers catch fire, dragonflies draw flame;
As tumbled over rim in roundy wells
Stones ring; like each tucked string tells, each hung bell's
Bow swung finds tongue to fling out broad its name;
Each mortal thing does one thing and the same;
Deals out that being indoors each one dwells;
Selves — goes itself; myself *it speaks and spells,*
Crying What I do is me: for that I came.

I say more: the just man justices;
Keeps grace; that keeps all his goings graces;
Acts in God's eye what in God's eye he is –
Christ – for Christ plays in ten thousand places,
Lovely in limbs, and lovely in eyes not his
To the Father through the features of men's faces.
                                                    (Gerard Manley Hopkins)

"For thou wilt light my candle: the LORD my God will enlighten my darkness." (Psalm 18.28, Authorized Version)

CATCHING
FIRE

E.A. VARLEY

BIBLE SOCIETY

British and Foreign Bible Society
Stonehill Green, Westlea, Swindon SN5 7DG, England

A catalogue record for this book is available from the British Library

ISBN 0 564 084158

Printed in Great Britain by Biddles Ltd, Guildford
Cover design and internal illustrations by Jane Taylor

CONTENTS

FOR ALAN NUGENT –
who lights candles

FOREWORD

WHY ARE YOU READING THIS BOOK?

Maybe you've just been asked to take on responsibility for some piece of adult education in your church — run a Lent course, lead a housegroup, train people to read the Bible in worship, or whatever — and you're hoping this book will give you some sense of how to go about it. You could be in ordained ministry, and looking for some suggestions of ways to develop an adult education policy that fits the particular needs of your church. You might be a member of your church council, interested in the responsibilities you share for looking at how your church assists the learning of its adult members. Perhaps you serve on its education committee (or are thinking about suggesting it forms an education committee). Or you could be an experienced educator of Christian adults, on the lookout for new ideas that you can take over and use in your own style for your own events. You might not have any particular practical motive. You might just like reading about adult Christian learning.

Whoever you are, one thing is certain: *you are an experienced learner.* All your life you have been taking in new information and gaining new insights. Human beings learn all the time, and the more you learn, the better able to learn you become. What we learn has effects on the way we shape our lives. It is only because we are skilled learners that we can cope with circumstances we have never faced before. Learning is as necessary to us as breathing.

A growing church is always meeting new challenges and new opportunities — nobody has ever tried to be the Church for your time and your place until now. Your collective learning skills are what lets you weigh up new situations and adapt to them. A church that can't respond to the unexpected is on the way to becoming a fossil: "where there is no vision, the people perish" (Proverbs 29.18, Authorized Version).

This book is written in the belief that all of us are "learning in faith" all the time, whether or not we realize it: not because of own own cleverness, but because of the ceaseless loving activity of God. We are the followers of a master who constantly goes on ahead of us into the "Galilee" of our own everyday lives. God our

Father is a living God, always at work among his children, surprising us with chances to work alongside him for peace and joy, wholeness and justice in this world he made and loves. The Spirit of Truth is our teacher, leading us on into all truth. You may catch fire eagerly at the Lord's touch, you may be dragged kicking and screaming; but there is no escape from the learning process.

In the Christian community, quite a lot of the work of educating adults is done by children, and even more by teenagers. Among us, too, God "...has given some to be apostles, some prophets, some evangelists, some pastors and teachers, to equip God's people for work in his service, for the building up of the body of Christ" (Ephesians 4.11–12).

Above all, we are people of the Bible. Working with the Bible is probably the most powerful means Christians have for understanding who God wants them to be and what that means in practice. We too, with all our faults and limitations, are "...fellow–citizens with God's people, members of God's household...built on the foundation of the apostles and prophets, with Christ Jesus himself as the corner–stone" (Ephesians 2.19–20).

We have the best of all possible reasons for wanting to learn about the people whose lives and choices are told in Scripture. They are our colleagues in faith. No less than they, we too are part of the continuing adventure of Immanuel, God with us, God through Christ Jesus present in the midst of his people. That is the basis for all our learning.

Each of this book's seven chapters ends with a Bible study reflecting on the chapter's subject matter. Two consider texts from the Gospels, one from Acts, the rest from the Bible Jesus himself used and loved, our Old Testament. You could work through the Bible studies on your own, but doing them with other people would be a much richer experience. If you are able to take up the suggestion in Chapter One of forming an education team to serve your church, or even better to serve several neighbouring churches, then that would be an ideal group to tackle the Bible studies together. If not, do you perhaps belong to a housegroup, cell group or clergy fraternal which might be interested?

EDUCATING CHRISTIAN ADULTS

Chapter One examines what a "Christian adult educator" does. What is involved? What qualities are needed? What can Jesus' practice teach us? How do you choose, train and support leaders? What management structure will work best for your church? How do you assess the effectiveness of your work?

WHAT COUNTS AS "ADULT CHRISTIAN EDUCATION"?

Educating Christian adults means finding ways to stimulate and support adult Christian learning. That involves much more than just setting up housegroups or laying on courses. Organized activities labelled "Christian education" are one small tributary in a vast river of (sometimes unnoticed) Christian learning. Adult Christian education helps the learning flow.

The chief educator of Christian adults is the Holy Spirit. It is no pious cliché to say that God is ceaselessly at work in the lives of all his children; it is a fact. There are no "ordinary people". In the right setting every adult has a remarkable history to'tell. Each is a uniquely gifted child of God, travelling through life, with all the new light and changing circumstances which that journey brings. Learning comes as each tests his or her experiences by the fire of faith.

Adult Christian education also involves much more than individual lives of faith. What each person learns only makes full sense within the one living body, the Church. God's household with its many mansions is present wherever two or three come together in the name of Jesus. It is a community of fellow–learners "growing in the knowledge and love of God", called to worship, serve and witness together to God's faith in humankind.

Education isn't a one–off pump–priming exercise to fit us for adult responsibilities, but a lifelong adventure. Adult Christians work out their discipleship by grappling with the choices they must make, using their time, money and abilities in the specific practical circumstances of each day. They learn from reflecting on what they have done and experienced, alone with God, or in the light of the Bible, or in a group with others. They learn from listening to others and answering their questions. They learn through wrestling with God in prayer, worship and God–talk (theology, if you prefer it in Greek), and from tapping the huge reservoir of Christian tradition; they can learn both by agreeing with what they are told and by disagreeing with it.

Christians are called to "expect the unexpected". Deep insights into spiritual reality come from the unlikeliest people; our most profound and life–changing learnings often happen without warning, in situations we never saw as "educational". The more people advance in holiness, the nearer they approach to the self–giving humility of God that pays close, loving attention to every person, every creature, every encounter. True Christian maturity means becoming truly able to learn.

THE ROLE OF THE ADULT CHRISTIAN EDUCATOR

Like Eli advising the child Samuel in the Temple (1 Samuel 3.1–9), the chief task of educators of adult Christians is to help people attune themselves to God, to hear the voice that speaks in unexpected ways — and like Eli, the educator may then have much to learn from the learner about what that voice is saying.

"You know that among the Gentiles the recognized rulers lord it over their subjects, and the great make their authority felt. It shall not be so with you; among you, whoever wants to be great must be your servant, and whoever wants to be first must be the slave of all." (Mark 10.42 –44)

What does being an educator mean to you? What do you think you are taking on, when you accept responsibility for helping your fellow adults to learn?

Glance down this list and mark any which particularly appeal to you as descriptions of your role in educating others. (The spaces at the bottom are for adding your own suggestions.)

Tutor	Teacher	Supervisor	Lecturer
Arsonist	Enchanter	Carpenter	Family doctor
Entertainer	Superhero	Ringmaster	Storyteller
Ladder	Conduit	Conductor	Librarian
Enabler	Facilitator	Animator	Co–ordinator
Director	Marshal	Navigator	Critic
Tree surgeon	Treasure hunter	Ploughman	Woman at the well
_____	_____	_____	_____
_____	_____	_____	_____

What does that say about your hopes and expectations for adult Christian learning activities?

- Are there any roles that you feel an educator of Christian adults should refuse to take?

- Why?

- Could there be ways of interpreting your task as an educator which hindered the learning of others?

It makes some difference whether you see educating adults chiefly in terms of:
- you providing them with *information* they did not previously have;

- you providing *structures* within which to examine what they already know;

- you and them together *discovering* things none of you had seen before.

All three are essential, but it is likely that you will have a personal order of preference between them. Your own gifts may be chiefly those of a communicator, or a designer, or an interpreter. One advantage of team leadership is that you can look for colleagues to work with, whose gifts complement yours.

Providing information is an important part of the educator's task — people will feel cheated if you leave them knowing no more at the end of a session than they did at the beginning. This does not necessarily mean "telling them things". There are many ways to pass on the flame of knowledge.

Beware of devaluing the knowledge, experience and skills which the fellow–adults you are working with already possess. Telling people what you think they ought to hear can be a hit–or–miss process: some of your hearers may be wondering why you think it is worth saying something so obvious, others could be totally out of their depth.

Inviting the members of the learning group to pool whatever thoughts they have about the subject under discussion is not only a good way to check out where you're starting from: since one person's old hat can be another's startling new insight, it can also be a good way of providing information!

Try beginning a study session with a quiz or questionnaire. Draw up a few simple, clear questions that will bring out the information you want people to have, and ask the group to tackle them individually or with a partner before comparing answers. You can fill in any gaps yourself.

Creative resources such as pictures, poems and music can inform the group's learning in an open, flexible way. These don't have to be established classics: children's art, a local writing group's poetry, or simple music–making can all be very powerful in the right setting.

Providing structure is another important responsibility. People trusting you with the leadership of their learning have the right to expect something that is within their capabilities and linked to their existing knowledge and concerns, but is also stimulating, challenging and leads them into new territory.

Skilled event design can give people the confidence to share their own insights, by putting them on ground where they have real expertise to offer, then helping them make the connections with Christian belief and practice; by showing the familiarity of what seemed strange, or by revealing new depths in what seemed familiar.

Beware of assuming that if you get the structure right, the learning will take care of itself. Adult learning is rather like a fluorescent–strip light bulb — however good your design is, it takes an initial jolt of energy before the whole thing lights up. On a good day the energy will come easily; but in the end this is a matter of grace not law. A wise designer will always have a few extra resources to hand, just in case...

Discovering together happens anyway — it's a poor cook who can't lick her own finger. One of the great perks of educating Christian adults, is the extraordinary range of learning opportunities you gain in the process.

If you have enjoyed more educational privileges than the people you are working with, that gives you resources they will very likely want you to share. If you are willing to explore rather than dictate, their questions can cut new facets on the gem of knowledge you are studying together, teaching you things you never realized you knew.

Beware of becoming so fascinated by your own discoveries that you forget what the aim of the event was supposed to be. It takes discernment to tell which insights can fruitfully be fed into the discussion then and there, and which are best kept to yourself for pondering over afterwards. It's a good sign if group members are chipping in eagerly with their own comments and questions, and a hazard sign if you find yourself doing more and more talking, and less and less listening.

JESUS AS AN ADULT EDUCATOR

Jesus and All-age Learning

In the normal human way, Jesus began teaching adults before he was born. Joseph found his ideas about righteousness in human relationships turned inside out by God (Matthew 1.18–25); Elizabeth learned the full implications of her own son's ministry (Luke 1.39–45); Mary, as the Life of the World grew within her, found her whole understanding of who she was and what her life meant revolutionized. As for the effect on their families, friends and neighbours, we can only guess. For many adults today also, pregnancy or approaching fatherhood are powerful learning experiences which lead to a deeper faith, or even to finding faith for the first time.

As a tiny baby Jesus already brought good news (babies often do). Matthew's astrologers (Matthew 2.1–12) and Luke's shepherds (Luke 2.8–20) found God at work in their lives in a new way, making fresh sense of all that they believed in. Mary "…treasured up all these things and pondered over them" (Luke 2.19) — "…and you too will be pierced to the heart," Simeon warned her (Luke 2.35).

By the time he was twelve, Jesus had mastered the timeless adolescent vocation of upsetting adult certainties. His parents "found him sitting in the temple surrounded by the teachers, listening to them and putting questions" (Luke 2.46). Any adult who has ever been floored by ruthless twelve–year–old moral insight will sympathise with those teachers.

Even as a young man (he was killed before he reached middle age), Jesus kept a powerful sense of how much children can teach adults. "Then he took a child, set him in front of them, and put his arm round him. 'Whoever receives a child like this in my name,' he said, 'receives me; and whoever receives me, receives not me but the One who sent me.'" (Mark 9.36–37)

Jesus as Teacher

All four gospels describe Jesus as a "teacher" (*didaskalos*), and "Teacher" was one of the most common titles by which people addressed him: his disciples, the religious establishment, strangers in the crowd. Virtually all his short public ministry was adult education of one kind or another.

He was *always ready to teach:* in synagogues, in the Temple, in private homes, in the streets, lighting people up (and upsetting some badly) by the way his words and actions opened the meaning of Scripture to them. People were struck by his air of authority (Mark 1.27, Matthew 7.29, Luke 4.32); "'How is it,' they said, 'that this untrained man has such learning?'" (John 7.14)

He *knew his Bible* (our Old Testament) comprehensively. His teaching uses biblical references in a rich, layered way.[1] When people tried to floor him with regulations based on literalist understandings of Scripture, he answered by pointing them to the text's wider context in the will of God, and to overarching principles of love in action (e.g. Matthew 12.1–8, 15.1–9).

He was more concerned to reveal the Father's glory than to teach a body of facts. He characteristically *taught in parables:* beautifully simple and memorable stories carrying an extraordinarily rich burden of meaning for anyone with their ears open. His teaching method, set out classically in Luke 10.25–8, was to bat questions back to the person who asked them, and meet demands for plain answers with another parable.

Downtrodden, lost, broken and unacceptable people, Jesus always treated with great respect. He pointed out the heroism of humble people as an example to the learned and successful: the prostitute braving a Pharisee's scorn to anoint Jesus' feet (Luke 7.36–50), the widow making her Temple offering with the last of her savings (Mark 12.41–44). He showed endless patience with those who knew they were sinners: "he will not snap off a broken reed, nor snuff out a smouldering wick, until he leads justice on to victory" (Matthew 12.20). Anger blazed up in him when he saw religious leaders treating the humble of the land as worthless (e.g. Luke 13.10–17), or making holiness a status–symbol (e.g. Matthew 23.1–39). He was just as tough on the professional theologians: "Alas for you lawyers! You have taken away the key of knowledge. You did not go in yourselves, and those who were trying to go in, you prevented." (Luke 11.52)

Jesus and the Disciples

The healing, forgiveness and reconciliation Jesus brought to people always challenged them to start life over again, renewed in hope.

He called particular disciples to travel with him, learn from him in a more concentrated way, and be sent out to share in his work.[2] As an adult education exercise, this was a qualified success: all four gospels agree that the disciples often missed the point of what he was saying, but it laid sound foundations for the Christian Church.

At his last meal with them before his betrayal he gave them the Eucharist — most powerful of learning tools: the means to bring Jesus himself into our very inmost being. Raised from the dead, he gave them the most glorious gift of all: the Holy Spirit, guide, comforter and friend.

WHAT QUALITIES DOES AN ADULT EDUCATOR NEED?

In fact God can (and does) use anyone as an educator of adults, under the right circumstances.

When you recruit leaders for your church's educational activities, the key qualifications, taking Jesus as our inspiration, are probably:

* *willingness to respond* to what people ask you for: guidance, information or a good verbal tussle;

* *knowing your Bible,* but being always ready to discover new depths;

* *the knack of finding words* that stay in people's minds;

* *respect for everyone,* particularly for people who see themselves as ill-educated and unimportant;

* and last but not least, a readiness to *stand up to powerful characters* in the interests of justice for all.

The best way to recruit a training/education team for your church is quite simply to keep a weather eye open for people who prove able to illuminate other people's faith experience. Don't be too sure you know what gifts you are looking for. It isn't necessarily the clever, well–educated people who are best able to spark off real learning in others. In the end, what makes a good adult educator is a mystery of shared grace.

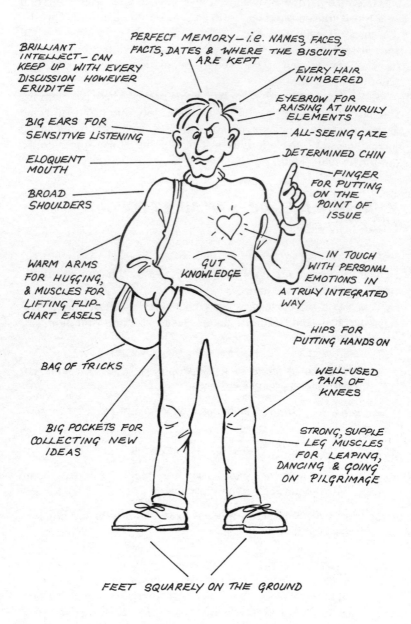

PERFECT MEMORY— i.e. NAMES, FACES, FACTS, DATES & WHERE THE BISCUITS ARE KEPT

BRILLIANT INTELLECT— CAN KEEP UP WITH EVERY DISCUSSION HOWEVER ERUDITE

EVERY HAIR NUMBERED

EYEBROW FOR RAISING AT UNRULY ELEMENTS

BIG EARS FOR SENSITIVE LISTENING

ALL-SEEING GAZE

ELOQUENT MOUTH

DETERMINED CHIN

FINGER FOR PUTTING ON THE POINT OF ISSUE

BROAD SHOULDERS

GUT KNOWLEDGE

WARM ARMS FOR HUGGING, & MUSCLES FOR LIFTING FLIP- CHART EASELS

IN TOUCH WITH PERSONAL EMOTIONS IN A TRULY INTEGRATED WAY

HIPS FOR PUTTING HANDS ON

BAG OF TRICKS

WELL-USED PAIR OF KNEES

BIG POCKETS FOR COLLECTING NEW IDEAS

STRONG, SUPPLE LEG MUSCLES FOR LEAPING, DANCING & GOING ON PILGRIMAGE

FEET SQUARELY ON THE GROUND

The knees and ears are crucial; pick and mix from the rest as you will.

If you have "education professionals" (teachers, trainers, lecturers and so forth) in your church, they are likely to be a genuine treasure to your education team. But you do occasionally find professionals who are so sure of what they want to teach, that they have little sensitivity to what people want to learn.

Calling unlikely people on to your team of educators falls into line with the gospels. We are servants of a God who "...has cast down the mighty from their thrones: and has lifted up the lowly. He has filled the hungry with good things: and the rich he has sent away empty" (*Magnificat*). Everyone knows they can learn from professors. Christians also have a lot to learn from those such as school lollipop ladies with no formal educational qualifications at all. Some adult Christians find great problems with organized learning activities because they don't see themselves as "clever enough". By being who they are, "uneducated" people can exercise educational ministries of great liberating power in a way not open to their more formally qualified colleagues.

If you recruit a strong lay team, will there also be a satisfying role for the clergy? Many ordained Christians enjoy working as educators, for instance preparing people for adult membership or marriage, leading housegroup sessions, delivering Lenten addresses. How can you negotiate to ensure that, as far as possible, everyone has a rewarding part to play?

Similarly, if unlikely people prove to have exceptional gifts for educational leadership, how will you help your professional educators cope with any feelings of rejection and jealousy they may experience?

TRAINING YOUR EDUCATION TEAM

It is easier to develop a tradition of drawing new people into leadership if you cultivate *team–led events* rather than solo leadership. This has a number of advantages:

* inexperienced leaders can begin by working in partnership with old hands;

* the team can balance different voices: men and women, older and younger people, more and less highly educated, "posh" and "working–class", different racial or ethnic groups, radical and conservative...;

* people can learn from each other's strengths and weaknesses.

If you want a team rather than a collection of individuals, they will
need to spend time getting to know and trust each other.

What are We About?

Start by asking each team member to talk at some length
(say 3–5 minutes) about their own education as an adult. This
is your chance to get them thinking about *all* the different
ways in which they learn, not just the organized courses they
have (or haven't) been on. For instance they might include
how they learned to do their job, or run a home, or be a par-
ent, or maintain a car; how they keep in touch with the news;
what they've learned through personal crises...

What common themes emerge from what is said? Try to build
up as full a picture as you can of the different ways adults
learn. You may like to write up the results on a large sheet of
paper, as an aid to seeing what you are saying. Which of the
learning paths identified are most relevant to your work
together as an education team?

What do you feel you are, and aren't, able to offer to your
church? Are there things people want but you can't offer? Are
there things you'd like to offer which nobody seems to want?

End by pooling your main strengths as a team. What do you
feel good about? anxious about? frustrated by? encouraged
by?

A good education team can offer each other:

- *support and encouragement* through listening to each other's
  ideas, hearing about each other's successes and mishaps, sym-
  pathizing where necessary, and sharing a vision of what might
  be achieved;

- *informed feedback* on how they are doing, individually and col-
  lectively, and how the events they run work out in practice;

- a *think tank* for tossing around new ideas, thrashing out shared
  principles, and trying out unfamiliar methods before they use
  them with others;

- *help with priorities,* and consolation for all the good ideas that fall by the wayside through lack of time or money.

If you have no possibility of forming a team and must work on your own, you will need to think about who might give you that kind of help. Are there people in your church, or in neighbouring churches, or even sympathetic people with no attachment to any church, who would be willing to act as members of an "education support group", though not (yet?) to join an education team?

Drawing people with no church commitment into your education work can be highly rewarding. They can help preserve you from excessive "churchiness"; they can guide you in setting up educational programmes with genuine appeal for people outside the Church as well as for the active membership; they can sharpen up your thinking by challenging you to say what you mean in ordinary language rather than woolly religious jargon. It does happen that they also discover the Lord Jesus for themselves, somewhere along the road.

EVALUATING YOUR WORK

Evaluation is easiest where your work has clear aims — then you can start by asking how far your aims were met.

Assessment Questions for a Learning Venture

Do you feel satisfied with the way it went? Were there any particularly good moments? Any particularly bad moments?

What have you picked up about the participants' reactions? Do you feel people enjoyed it? Did they learn from it? What taste did it leave in their mouths? If you included any participant evaluation in your design, what does it show?

Were the aims met? Were they clear enough? Did they prove to be the right aims for the occasion?

Was the advance planning satisfactory? Did the practical arrangements cover everything they needed to? Was every member of the leadership team adequately briefed?

> Is there anything to learn from what happened during the venture?
>
> Does anything now need following up?

If some event or exercise goes particularly badly, you could learn a great deal from asking yourselves why. There's nothing like a really good resounding failure for teaching you your job.

MANAGEMENT STRUCTURES

How is the education work managed in your church? Who plans the learning activities, monitors their overall balance, supervises their finances, evaluates their effectiveness, recruits leaders and sees to their training, checks out the educational implications of church policy decisions and does the long–term planning ?

There are advantages to involving non–educators in the management, rather than simply leaving it all to the clergy or the education team.

* You can bring the *user viewpoint* into planning. You experience events differently when you are leading them. Participants can offer important insights into what you are doing.

* You are *guarded against becoming too cosy,* inward–looking and wrapped up in your own jargon (provided you don't just domesticate your non–educators into joining in!)

* You can bring in *other kinds of expertise* — financial or artistic, for example.

Do you have an education committee? Do you need one, or do you feel better served by leaving it as the Church Council's responsibility? Does the Church Council have time to do justice to all that is involved?

If you do want an education committee, who might serve on it?

* Will the *clergy* be ex–officio members? If not, how will you ensure that they are kept well briefed about its activities, and also that the work remains in the mainstream of church life?

- Will the *education team members* be ex–officio? If so, will recruiting a large team make the committee size unmanageable? If not, how will you ensure good communications and avoid power struggles between committee and team?

- What people with *useful skills or expertise* might be invited to serve? Are there people who are too busy to be regular members, but willing to be consulted for advice and drawn into particular projects?

- Can you find at least one *good, gritty non–expert* who will constructively criticise from an outsider's perspective? Will this person provide the *user viewpoint* in your planning? If not, who will?

What will be the committee's terms of reference? Will it be given total oversight, or asked to perform specific functions and report back to the Church Council? Will you share the management tasks between different bodies: the clergy team, the education team, the committee, the council? If so, how will they be allocated, and co–ordinated?

What scope is there for submitting the overall education work of your church to the consideration of the whole membership? Is an annual report produced? Who receives it, and how is it presented? Is the education programme ever given space at the annual church meeting, or other major occasion in church life?

LIVING ON A LARGER MAP

Don't keep your educational vision penned up inside your own boundaries.

What resources does your own denomination make available for educational work, locally, regionally and nationally? Is there a local or regional register of people with teaching and training skills? Can you use this expertise in some way — and should you be offering the skills of your own church's education team more widely?

How about the *other denominations?* What scope is there for organizing your learning events ecumenically, either at neighbourhood or district level? Could you interest a neighbourhood group of churches in forming a joint education team?

Might a local *college, university* or *educational association*
(such as the WEA) be interested in joint courses? Could you
co–operate with your area's Health Education unit, or share learning resources with a Citizen's Advice Bureau?

What local voluntary organizations might you build educational
links with?

Bear in mind the possibilities for taking part in wider debate.
Periodicals such as *Education in Church Today, Adult Network*
and the *Journal of Theological Education* can help you stay
abreast of new developments in adult Christian learning. You may
find interesting things emerging from your own work, that you
would like to share with fellow–practitioners: journals can be con-
tributed to as well as read. If you have a denominational mailing,
the editor might be glad of the occasional article on education
issues — especially if one of your team has a gift for writing vivid
punchy prose.

Networking with other people who share your interests, is
another good source of stimulation and encouragement. Networks
have grown up around many areas of adult education, from
Christians in Public Life to Participatory Bible Study. Your
denomination's national education department should be able to
advise you on what is currently available.

BIBLE STUDY

*"But, LORD," Moses protested, "I have never been a man of
ready speech, never in my life, not even now that you have
spoken to me; I am slow and hesitant." The LORD said to
him, "Who is it that gives man speech? Who makes him
dumb or deaf? Who makes him keen–sighted or blind? Is it
not I, the LORD? Go now; I shall help you to speak and show
you what to say." Moses said, "LORD, send anyone else you
like." At this the LORD became angry with Moses: "Do you
not have a brother, Aaron the Levite? He, I know, will do all
the speaking. He is already on his way out to meet you, and
he will be overjoyed when he sees you. You are to speak to
him and put the words in his mouth; I shall help both of you
to speak and tell you what to do."* (Exodus 4.10–15)

1. Read the passage aloud. What tone of voice do you think Moses is speaking in? How about God? Do you find it easy or difficult to think of God as having a voice? Do you ever have experiences you could call "hearing God speak"?

2. Moses was panicked by the thought of having to speak up in public. What are your main horrors and anxieties about setting out to educate your fellow Christian adults? If you protested about that to God, what do you think God's reply would be, judging by this text?

3. God sent Aaron to help Moses with the part of his mission that he most dreaded. How must Moses have felt about having to rely on his brother like that? Does that spark anything about your own situation? Do you rely on other people to cover areas where you are weak?

4. Moses received particular gifts to help in the work God entrusted to him. What are your major gifts for aiding other people's learning? (No false modesty!) Ask friends who know you well and will speak their minds (not say what they think you want to hear) what your strengths are. How do you intend using, and developing, these strengths?

5. God promised Moses and Aaron, "I shall help both of you to speak and tell you what to do." Do you feel you can rely on God to guide your work in the same way? How?

Notes

1. For instance in the parable of the vineyard (Mark 12.1–12 and parallels) his words stand on their own, but placing the reference to Isaiah 5.1–7 fills in extra levels of meaning.
2. Luke 8.1–3 and Mark 15.40–41 say that some who travelled with him were women.

PREPARING THE GROUND

Chapter Two concerns the preparation work needed for effective learning. How do you take stock of all the different ways learning already goes on in your church? Where are the best opportunities for new work? How can you help keep your church a lively, stimulating place where learning comes naturally? What resources of buildings and equipment do you have?

WHERE ARE YOU STARTING FROM?

When you first begin work as an educator with adult Christians, you could be tempted to feel you are starting from scratch — particularly if you know these people, or even your whole local church, have "never done any adult education before".

Don't you believe it! God is absolutely guaranteed to have got in ahead of you. What you *are* likely to find, though, is that people don't give themselves credit for all the learning they are doing. Many Christians seem rather like the man who hadn't realized he was writing prose. They don't count the things life has taught them as "education"; it would not occur to them to call their understanding of God "theology".

There are at least two reasons why people discount most of the education they receive as adult Christians:

- they often take a narrow view of the word "education". For "education" you have to take part in special formal activities, with an accredited person to teach you. Yet down the ages, the "University of Life" has turned out more saints than all the other universities put together.

- people can feel it is only the "religious" part of their experience — formal worship, Bible study, prayer, being taught about the faith — that counts as being Christian.

One of the biggest joys of an adult educator's ministry is helping people discover just how rich their history already is. Like the Wise Men, they have plenty of treasures in their luggage to lay at Jesus' feet.

DISORGANIZED LEARNING

Because the Holy Spirit has ultimate charge of your church's learning programme, a whole lot happens in informal, unorganized ways.

People meet and talk, in the street, in the supermarket queue, in the bar, at the school gate, over coffee after the Sunday service.

* They exchange *news,* and the church keeps in touch with what is happening in the community — within the church family, and wider: joyful happenings to be celebrated; problems to be tackled; personal sorrows to be respected; opportunities to offer comfort, help or consolation in the name of Christ.

* They ask each other for *advice,* and quietly, without making a big issue of it, build up each other's effectiveness as Christ's servants in their own corner of the world.

* They talk about things that have illumined them, or discouraged, or baffled them. Swapping different *points of view,* they find new insights and understandings. New Christians pick up the fruits of what their more experienced colleagues have learned through years of struggling to understand, serve and witness. Established Christians are challenged by the vision and eagerness to learn of those for whom faith in Jesus is an exciting new discovery.

Life experiences test and change people's faith. You become officially adult at eighteen, and may well go on being an adult for sixty, seventy or more years. That's a long time. During adulthood people experience an enormous range of significant changes.

* Our *working lives* present plenty of challenges: finding paid employment (or failing to); practical dilemmas about what it means to do your work in a Christian way; coping with promotion and greater responsibilities, or with disappointment at not being offered promotion; changing jobs and moving to new places; spending time out of work to raise a family, or care for ageing parents, or through redundancy and unemployment, then maybe starting afresh; facing up to retirement.

* Through *relationships* with other people we learn the complexities of loving acceptance, shared joy and shared pain, hurt and rejection, bereavement, grief and loss. We learn to "forgive those who trespass against us", and to seek forgiveness for our

own trespasses. Some take the way of marriage and parenthood, with all that involves. Some take other paths, and brave the pressure of society to conform.

Then there's the whole area of *public education*. There are books, magazines, journals, newspapers, television and radio. All the churches produce reports to keep their members informed on major issues of concern. Christian Aid and its sister development agencies have public development education programmes aimed at putting us more closely in touch with the needs, lives and faith of our partners in the many economically deprived countries of the world. Charities and campaigning groups leaflet us through the letterbox about their areas of interest. As adult Christians in this society, we have access to huge resources for informal, self-organized learning about ourselves, our world and our Christian faith.

In any church, the wealth of experience and insight people have gained from their "education so far", formal and informal, is a major learning resource. The Church's most important educational task is to provide settings in which people can chew this over in the light of the Bible and of Christian truth, in order to take a firmer grasp on their faith.

The activities you arrange need to:

* meet people's real learning priorities;
* fit in with the church's whole programme.

Finding out what is already happening can be a learning opportunity in itself. Why not try a *stocktaking evening* and bring together a representative sample of people to help build up a picture of your church's existing learning activities?

Stocktaking Evening

Give it the special occasion treatment — meet somewhere with good facilities, and take a bit of trouble with the refreshments. It all helps to emphasize that this is valuable and serious work you are engaged on.

It is important to come at the task from a broad view of "what counts as adult education". Why not begin by asking everyone to take a minute of silence and think about one recent occasion when they really felt they had learned something?

After a minute or two, ask people to tell the group about their own occasion. Don't just go round the circle — invite people to speak when they feel ready. This encourages them to listen carefully to each other, rather than sit back waiting for their turn to come.

This is not the moment to start talking over what has been said. The point is to give everyone present a chance to speak from their own experience, and be listened to without question. Make sure nobody is accidentally missed out, although anyone who is really unwilling to say anything can simply keep silent.

When everyone has spoken, take a few minutes to sum up the different kinds of learning that have been mentioned. Is that a complete picture of the ways adults learn? Do any other important kinds of learning opportunity spring to mind?

Next, ask people to talk with the person next to them about where they feel learning is going on in the life of your church at the present time. What organized learning activities are there? Where is "unorganized learning" happening? Who is involved? Who is left out?

In a large group it's useful to give everyone a scribblesheet (see p. 37) for keeping notes on, and taking away afterwards as a record of the discussion.

When the conversations begin to run down, ask what results people have come up with. Write up their answers on a flipchart, whiteboard or strip of newsprint. Allow plenty of time for people to look the results over and fill in the gaps.

A useful way to build up a picture of your situation is to begin with a large crude outline drawing of a church building. Inside the outline write up all the learning activities, formal and informal, regular and occasional, that go on in church, or in the church hall. Outside the church outline write up all the learning opportunities people enjoy in other places (homes, workplaces, leisure activities, hospitals and so on) which you feel are worth including.

> When you all feel that you have noted the significant current learning activities in your church, take some time just to look at the resulting picture. How do you feel about what you have described? Do you see any particular strengths — or any particular weaknesses? Can you see opportunities that might be made more of — dangers to watch out for?
>
> The evening could appropriately end with a time of prayer. You might offer all these learning activities to God, pray for any particular needs or opportunities, give thanks for the constant work of the Holy Spirit leading us all deeper into truth.

Now that you have your picture, where will you take it? Would your deacons' or elders' meeting, or standing committee, find it a useful starting point for discussing policy? How about the clergy, and ministerial team if you have one?

STRUCTURES FOR LEARNING

Having looked into the current state of adult education in your church, do you find the way your learning activities are organized is logical and helpful? Are you satisfied that:

• *new Christians* are getting the basic teaching they need, in a form they can readily relate to?

• *established Christians* have enough opportunities to work together on the issues that concern them, and are being offered fresh insights to keep their faith alive and growing?

• *all–age learning* is alive and well, and open to anyone willing to join in? Are all your mixed–age activities seen as learning opportunities for the adults involved?

• there are no groups whose learning needs are being overlooked?

• there are no people working separately or in isolation who would be better off learning together?

• communications are good — everyone knows what opportunities are available and how to get in?

Have you found any areas of work that might benefit from being *overhauled?* For instance if you have a housegroup system, how does it function? How are people allocated to housegroups? Who attends the different housegroups, and do significant groups within the congregation hold aloof? If the housegroups seem only to have limited appeal, can you tell why? Are the meeting times convenient for everyone? Are some people genuinely too busy to take on any more commitments? Are there any problems about the way the housegroups are set up, or the way meetings are organized? Are the housegroup leaders properly supported — and by whom?

Do you see any particular needs for *new work?* There is a limit to the number of learning activities any church can organize. Overhauling your education policy may mean launching new ventures — or strengthening what is being done already — or even bringing some activities to an end.

This exercise is a useful way to help a lively group look at how they want their church's educational policy to develop:

Burning Bush

Prepare coloured–paper cut–out twigs, buds, and flowers and give everyone a handful of each. Ask them to write on the flowers, what they think are the finest learning activities going on in your church at present — the ones that are most worthwhile. On the buds, ask them to write what they see as growth points. The twigs are for dead wood which ought to be cut out. Have a large drawing of a bush to stick the completed cut–outs on. The finished bush can be displayed somewhere people can see it easily, maybe inside the church building. It can then be thought about, talked about and prayed about over a period of time.

If you've managed to bring together a genuinely mixed group, and the members are being honest rather than saying what they think you want to hear, then you are likely to find a good deal of disagreement about strengths and weaknesses. One person's dead wood may well be another person's flower.

Dealing with dead wood is often the most difficult of issues for churches to face. You have wonderful plans for a new housegroup structure, but dear old Mrs So–and–so will be dreadfully upset if you shut down the discussion group that meets in her front room on second Thursdays, even though hardly anyone turns up, and those who do still make the effort are never quite sure what they are discussing.

This is a genuine difficulty, and there is no simple right answer to it. If you are faced with killing off the withered remains of somebody's pride and joy, then it probably will cause anguish and outrage. It is worth taking time and prayer to be sure that you really have found the right course of action; but good ventures with noble histories do reach their natural end: it could be a case of "no death — no Easter".

If your education committee or team faces one of those situations, this Bible reflection could help:

1. Have someone look up Judges 11 beforehand, and prepare a very short introduction explaining Jephthah's situation at the beginning of verse 34, including the information that, in order to win victory, Jephthah has promised God a sacrifice; and has left it up to God to choose what sacrifice the occasion demands.

2. After the introduction, someone reads Judges 11.34–40 aloud. Ask everyone to listen reflectively, then find the passage in their own Bibles. Each person now chooses to work on the text from the point of view of Jephthah, or his companions, or his daughter, or her friends. (If more than one person has chosen the same character/group to identify with, they might like to work together.)

3. Allow three or four minutes for people to mull over how their character or group would feel about what has happened, then share your insights together. Are any key themes highlighted?

4. When everyone has had their say, ask the group to reflect in silence for another three or four minutes on what lessons you might learn from this for handling your own very different situation. The silence is important for letting people follow their own trains of thought without interruption.

5. Finally, pool your thoughts and suggestions, and see if any agreement emerges as to what should be done.

With all the care and sensitivity in the world, and the most triumphant of successful outcomes, some people may still experience change as a terrible disaster. Mrs So-and-so may accept your case for the housegroup initiative, and agree on a good, respectful way to end the life of her discussion group, and become a committed supporter of the new system. Or she may refuse to listen; in extreme cases, people who feel their offering has been rejected can leave the church altogether. In the end you are very dependent on the grace of the people you work with. Although the grace of God has its way of getting involved too, all good adult education work carries an unavoidable element of risk.

LOW–KEY LEARNING

One useful way to make your church a richer learning environment is to look at what can be done through *informal, unorganized educational activities.*

There are many quiet but effective ways to improve the quality of education your church offers to its members, without large demands on people's time and energy.

Do you already produce a weekly notice sheet with information about the services and notices for the forthcoming week? Why not add a weekly "think spot" — a concise, vividly presented item of Christian interest to catch people's attention and make them think? This might be:

- a clear, striking explanation of some doctrinal point, e.g. "Salvation means..."

- a cartoon

- a piece discovered in a local or national newspaper

- a quote from a book or magazine

- a story you have heard, retold in your own words

- a poem or verse of an unfamiliar hymn

- a joke

- a biblical quotation

- a set of telling statistics

- a news item from an aid or mission agency

The possibilities are endless. Keep your "think spot" short — no more than about sixty words — and always acknowledge where you took it from. Use simple, lively graphics to make it stand out on the page. If you can't draw, buy in some copyright–free artwork. When using published material, be careful not to infringe the law: Jay Books produce a handy practical guide, *Understanding Copyright* by Eric A Thorn, ISBN no. 1–870404–03–3.

Does your congregation come together for *fellowship after worship?* If so, take a good look at the meeting place.

- Is it a comfortable, welcoming place, or a scruffy, dingy outpost full of broken chairs, dead flies and left–over jumble, cold in winter and stuffy in summer? What is the state of the meeting place telling people about the importance your church attaches to fellowship?

- Is there interesting, thought–provoking display material for people to look at while they drink their coffee?

- If there is, when was it last changed? People soon stop noticing a display that always looks just the same.

Three Wishes

For this activity you need a huge cut–out circle with a suitable part of the world roughly drawn on it, plus enough cut–out stars of assorted different colours for everyone to have three.

Each person is asked to think what three wishes they feel God would make for their own personal future, and write one wish on each of their three stars.

They are also invited to write on the globe, one wish they feel God would make for the future of his whole world.

The globe and stars can be stuck on a sheet of newsprint to make a mural, or hung up around the whole fellowship area as a vast mobile.

Try setting up a monthly rota of people willing to take their turn at creating something for others to look at. This might include: banners or posters; artwork produced by the Children's Church or Sunday School, particularly where they have been working on the same Scripture texts and themes as the adult members of the congregation; promotional material about local charities, or issues in the local community; information on other parts of the world Church, for instance through mission links; a display of pictures and objects associated with, say, prayer; a piece of "action art" where everyone is invited to make their own contribution, for example by decorating a cut–out figure to represent him– or herself and adding it to a collage scene of the whole church on the move.

Does your church already have a *bookstall?* If not, could you think about setting one up? Better still, could you find somebody else, or a small group of people, to do it for you? If you already have a bookstall, take a careful look to check you are making the most of it.

* Is it in a prominent place where it will catch people's eyes as they go about their normal church business? (Tuck it away in a dark nook, and people may never realize their church *has* a bookstall!)

* Is it well–sited for people to browse through at leisure, without causing traffic jams?

* Will your suppliers let you take interesting new books for a time on sale or return, so you can change the titles on the stall regularly without too much financial risk?

* Have you thought about selling posters, prayer cards, reproductions of religious art, thought–provoking greetings cards, or other aids to meditation? You will probably not be able to afford to stock everything you might like, but perhaps there could be special ventures at appropriate times of the year.

* How about occasionally inviting a specialist Christian publisher to put on an exhibition of their materials? Try your Christian Aid Area Secretary, Bible Society or Scripture Union representative; or approach a body such as Grove Booklets; or try your favourite publisher of children's religious books. You might consider linking this up with some major service or event shared with other neighbouring churches — or how about a grand Flower Festival and Book Fair combined ?

* Many churches run second–hand bookstalls during fund–raising activities. Why not try boosting your bookstall's educational effectiveness by sorting what comes in and giving pride of place to thought–provoking Christian books, non–fiction and fiction, rather than the latest pulp thrillers? (The thrillers will probably still sell fastest!) A well–designed stall display, perhaps with some inexpensive and carefully chosen new books on sale among the second–hand ones, can direct people's interest to good things they might otherwise pass over without notice.

TAKING STOCK OF YOUR RESOURCES

What *buildings* do you have use of for learning purposes?

• How flexible is your *church building?* Does it have pews or chairs? Is it easy to move around in, for the aged and creaky, as well as the young and athletic? Does it have wheelchair and pram access, good acoustics, a sound system, an induction loop for the hard of hearing? How much open space is there? Are there areas where small groups can work together? Is it well ventilated and warm in cold weather? Is there an adaptable lighting system with creative possibilities for highlighting particular areas? Are there accessible power points? Is it full of treasures that must not be touched or moved?

• Do you have a *church hall, or halls?* How big, and how welcoming are they? Are they sweet–smelling or frowsty? What are the heating and ventilation like? Is there sufficient lighting, and are there any power points? Are the floors suitable to sit and lie on (carpeted?)? Is there a raised stage area? Are there plenty of comfortable and adult–sized chairs? Are the tables large or small? Can the furniture be lifted without causing hernias? Are the walls suitable for display purposes? What is the access from the main church building like?

• Do you have *other meeting rooms?* How many, and what number can each comfortably accommodate? Straightforward access or all opening off each other? Within easy reach of your main working area? What state of decoration? What furnishings? Well–lit or gloomy? Natural daylight or perpetual electricity? Can the vestry (or vestries) be used for learning activities, and if so, how much clutter will have to be put up with?

• Do you have enough *toilets?* Are they in working order, clean, kept supplied with toilet paper, reasonably easy to find? Handwashing facilities, with soap and towels? Disabled access?

• Are there any *kitchen facilities?* Mains water supply? Somewhere to make and serve hot drinks, *and* wash up afterwards? Within easy reach of your main working areas? Does the church have its own kettle(s) or urn, teapot(s), cups and saucers (or mugs), milk jugs and sugarbowls, teaspoons, plates, other cutlery, a fridge for milk and a good–sized rubbish bin?

- Is there plenty of *storage space* for your training gear and supplies? Shelves and cupboards? Is there secure locked storage for valuable equipment? Who holds the keys, and are they always available when needed?

When you have collected all this information, review it (with the education committee if you have one) and see how well off you are. Are there any particular strengths you want to build into your future planning, or any big pluses you hadn't previously noticed? Are there any glaring lacks and deficiencies? Is there anything you can do about them right away, or in the longer term? Does your church have any building plans that you might be able to influence?

EQUIPMENT

Some commonly used items of training equipment:

- *Flipcharts* are large (usually size A1) sheets of paper, widely used by adult educators for writing up whatever they need to during educational activities. They are almost an emblem: a friend who once met me staggering to my car under the weight of two flipchart easels murmured, "Ah, flipcharts... Are you by any chance an Adult Education Officer?" (The friendship survived — just!) Flipcharts are a flexible and portable resource. When a sheet is full, you can stick it to a convenient nearby wall and people can still see what is on it.

  If your church doesn't already possess a flipchart easel, you might consider buying one. The kind that doubles as a whiteboard offers the most possibilities. Alternatively someone with an enthusiasm for DIY among the congregation might make you something perfectly suitable. Newsprint paper, if you can get it, is cheaper and can be cut to the size you want.

  Because a flipchart easel looks rather like a blackboard, it can give your working area an unfortunate schoolroom flavour. To avoid this, tuck the flipchart easel away somewhere inconspicuous until it is needed, and only bring it out when you are ready to use it. In a small group it is often better to put the flipchart paper on the table or floor rather than using an easel. This is particularly true if you want all the group members to write on it.

* *Overhead Projector* (OHP). Useful for working with very large groups, because the image can be blown up as big as your screen (or white wall) allows. This can prove an advantage when working with people whose eyesight is not brilliant, who often find it impossible to make out handwritten words on flipcharts at anything but point–blank range. OHP slides can be prepared beforehand to give a good professional–looking effect. If you have access to a photocopier, you can buy OHP acetates suitable for photocopying, and transfer printed text or drawings on to them. Given a few artistic skills and a lot of imagination, you can build up elaborate effects using overlays and shields. Beware of getting carried away, and letting the visual aid interest you more than what the participants are to do with it!

* *Blackboard/Whiteboard.* Blackboards create dust and mess, but chalk is much cheaper than whiteboard markers. Both blackboards and whiteboards can be very useful tools for recording the results of a learning session. They give plenty of scope for the participants to change their minds about what should be written: it is easy to rub out, rewrite and rearrange material until your findings are in a pleasing form. Their main disadvantage is giving no permanent record of what has been written, unless somebody copies it all down.

* *Cassette Recorder.* Tape cassettes have many uses. Just as radio plays can be a richer imaginative resource than television, so sound tapes can sometimes stimulate discussion more effectively than video. Well–chosen sound effects on tape are a powerful way to create atmosphere for Bible study, meditation or liturgical drama. The BBC publishes a vast range of sound effects.

* *Compact Disc* (CD). If you can afford the kind of portable equipment that plays compact discs, CDs have considerable advantages over tape for playing commercially recorded music. No more fumbling around beforehand trying to find the right track on the tape; no more being unable to use track 13 because you must have track 4 and there is no time to wind on in between. A CD player is generally programmable to play whatever tracks you want, in whatever order you want. Plus you won't find your favourite piece has stretched and gone out of tune due to heavy use, or been chewed and destroyed by ram-

paging toddlers (even jam wipes off CDs), nor that the end of the tape has come unstuck and disappeared inside the cassette. The big disadvantage of CDs is that you can't (at the time of writing) make your own recordings, so are dependent on what can be bought commercially.

- *Video.* Now that so many people own video recorders, most church groups should be able to use video tapes. Television being such a familiar learning medium, even the least confident people are often happy with educational videos. There are many excellent videos available, on everything from healing ministries to marriage preparation. There are also some execrably bad ones; it is worth watching before buying, if possible. A number of agencies will hire out videos as well as selling them, though some hire charges represent a large fraction of the selling price.

- *Slide Projector.* Tape–slide presentations are rather out of fashion, which is a pity. They are an accessible technology: stopping the tape for a longer consideration of the point being made is easy, with the slide to look at while you ponder. Most churches have the resources to make their own very effective tape–slides. Projecting appropriate slides also makes a highly effective focus for meditation exercises.

- *Photocopier.* This is one of the inventions that revolutionized adult Christian education; its uses are innumerable. Unless you have easy inexpensive access to photocopying facilities elsewhere, it could be worthwhile looking into the possibilities of acquiring one for your church. The leap in quality, and the time saved, by changing from duplicated to photocopied materials is vast, and the cost difference less than it used to be.

- *Word Processor.* If your church has not yet joined the computer revolution, it is worth considering taking the plunge. Your youth group should be able to advise you about the best hardware and software to go for!

BIBLE STUDY

> *Be glad, O people of Zion, rejoice in the LORD your God,*
> *for he has given you a teacher for righteousness.*
> *He sends you abundant showers,*
> *both autumn and spring rains as before.*
> *The threshing–floors will be filled with grain;*
> *the vats will overflow with new wine and oil.*
> *I will repay you for the years the locusts have eaten —*
> *the great locust and the young locust,*
> *the other locusts and the locust swarm —*
> *my great army that I sent among you.*
> *You will have plenty to eat, until you are full,*
> *and you will praise the name of the LORD your God,*
> *who has worked wonders for you;*
> *never again will my people be shamed.*
> *Then you will know that I am in Israel,*
> *that I am the LORD your God,*
> *and that there is no other;*
> *never again will my people be shamed.*
> *And afterwards, I will pour out my Spirit on all people.*
> *Your sons and daughters will prophesy,*
> *your old men will dream dreams,*
> *your young men will see visions.*
> *Even on my servants, both men and women,*
> *I will pour out my Spirit in those days.*
>
> (Joel 2.23–29, NIV)

1. Read the passage aloud, slowly, and savour the images it pre-
   sents. This is one of the most glorious visions in the whole of
   Scripture — no wonder it leapt to Peter's mind on the Day of
   Pentecost (Acts 2.16–18).

2. "The years that the locust has eaten…" What does that conjure
   up for you? Where in the life of your church are the areas of
   loss and damage and waste that you would most like to see
   repaid?

3. *Let there be, in some place,*
   a community of men, women, elderly, children, and new–born
   babies

as a first fruit, as our appetizer, and our embrace of the future...
(Rubem A. Alves, Brazil)

What kind of community do you long for the Church to become? Could you try to draw it? This isn't about producing great Art, but finding the images that express your hopes and dreams for a truly growing church. If you have the skills, you might even make a "Dreams and Visions" banner, and use it to share your vision with others.

4. When your drawing is near enough as you want it, take a few minutes to look at it, and reflect on how the various learning activities you are engaged in help to move your church in the direction of that vision. Do you want to make any changes to your drawing, in the light of these reflections? Do you want to make any changes to the learning activities?!

5. Finally, read the passage from Joel again and enjoy it. "He who calls you keeps faith; he will do it." (1 Thessalonians 5.24)

FOR THE WHOLE BODY

*Chapter Three is about learning events for the whole church con-
gregation together. How do you organize events for large, mixed
groups of people, all at different ages and stages in their Christian
development? What are the best ways to break big gatherings
down into groups of more manageable size, without losing the true
sense that everyone is working together? What kinds of occasion
call for whole–body consideration?*

WE'RE ALL IN THIS TOGETHER . . .

If learning activities are an important part of your church's life, it
matters that, so far as is humanly possible, everyone should feel
included. Otherwise, there is a risk of splitting into factions. "What
I mean is this: each of you is saying, 'I am for Paul,' or 'I am for
Apollos'; 'I am for Cephas,' or 'I am for Christ.' Surely Christ has
not been divided!" (1 Corinthians 1.12–13)

"Oh, he's in with John's bunch." "She's one of the minister/
vicar's henchpersons." "Those charismatics who huddle over at
Mary's place on Wednesdays..." "We faithful few are the real
Christians in this church." The kind of mistrust, suspicion and
inter–group rivalry that can grow up where a church's main learning activities are restricted to the lucky few, can undermine all that
your learning programme was meant to achieve.

The real frustration of trying to include everyone is, of course,
the difficulty of getting them to turn up. Modern people tend to
lead busy, complex lives with many different and competing priorities. However carefully you consult people before fixing a date,
however far in advance you announce it, however wonderful and
well–distributed your publicity, however regularly you remind
everyone about it, and however valuable what you are offering
may be, you are very likely to find some people missing on the
day. Never mind. Take a lead from the way God has dealt with his
people down the centuries. Work creatively with the ones who do
respond, and never give up scheming to get all the rest along as
well next time.

Cunning ways to draw in more people include:

- Make an attractive *children's/young people's programme* part of
  the event. Not just a bit of tacked–on childminding, but some-

thing the younger members of the congregation will really look forward to, and perhaps bring their friends to as well. It helps your event to be seen as a day out for the family rather than a grim duty.

- Set up your timetable so that it *leaves a useful part of the day free*. If you have chosen a Saturday, try beginning at noon or ending by 3 p.m. so that people can fit their normal Saturday things around your event.

- Choose an interesting venue. If your event takes people to a place they would really like to visit and leaves them some time free to look around, you might even persuade them to give up a Bank Holiday!

- Sunday Specials. Many people feel that Sundays are already given to the Church in any case, which can mean quite a positive reception for Sunday afternoon activities.

Sunday lunch is often still an important landmark. Plan a starting time that allows plenty of space after the end of morning worship for getting home, cooking, eating, washing–up and coming back. Or why not experiment with a shared fellowship meal as part of the event? A full cooked meal is probably worth the extra bother: people who value their Sunday lunch can be seriously disgruntled if they have to make do with a sandwich and sausage roll instead, and may find themselves physically unable to concentrate. However, the work involved needs careful organizing. It would be a shame to leave some members so tied up in providing food that they missed out on the main programme. You might even experiment with a design that makes the cooking, eating and washing–up learning activities in their own right!

LARGE AND SMALL GROUPS

Bringing the whole church body (or as much of it as will come!) together to work on a shared task presents a double challenge.

- First, *each member needs the chance to make his/her contribution effectively.*

- Second, *there must be a genuine sense that everyone is working together.*

The straightforward large group, everyone in together, is some-times called *working in plenary*. It has important uses. A well thought out plenary session can be one of the very best ways to help people work together effectively and enjoyably.

If you are designing a "whole body" event for your church, you will probably want to include plenary sessions:

1. *At the beginning,* so that everyone starts off together and hears the same introduction. If the participants begin by assembling in separate groups and being separately briefed, you will need to think very carefully about how you can enable them to end by feeling they have all been taking part in the same event.

2. *At the end,* to bring everything back together. This is the point at which to look for a shared understanding of what the event has achieved, and consider what next steps to take.

There may well be other points at which it makes most sense to be in plenary; for instance, listening to an invited speaker, taking part in a guided meditation, watching a visual presentation, or joining in a structured large–group exercise.

Primed Plenary

This helps people put their ideas in order and try them out on a partner before presenting them to the whole group in plenary.

Begin by giving everyone their own copy of a scribblesheet — that is, an A5 or A4 sheet with the question you want them to con-sider written in large clear letters. It is worth taking some trouble to get the question right: short, crisp and to the point. If you add some lines to write on, that makes the paper less threatening to look at, and also gives some idea of how many answers you expect them to come up with. An appropriate line drawing (your own or copyright–free artwork) adds to the friendlier appearance.

What do children value most about worship?

This is an example of a scribblesheet for starting off a study day on the theme "How can we find more effective ways to involve our children in worship?"

One way to use it would be by pairing each adult with a child (one of each makes a very interesting team) and ask them to work on the question together.

When you give out the scribblesheets (especially if you are not sure how literate everyone is), make it clear that they won't be collected in or marked. Each person's piece of paper is theirs to keep. When they have finished using it they can keep notes of the discussion on it; or doodle on it; or stare at it as an aid to concentration. Everyone is asked to scribble down their own ideas. After a few minutes, or when most people seem to have stopped writing, ask them to compare notes with the person sitting next to them. Finally, invite everyone to call out what they have written down. It often helps to write up the key words on a flipchart or overhead projector slide, particularly if you want the group to go on and work with the information.

This exercise is particularly useful in very large groups of thirty or more, and also in situations where it matters for everyone to have their own written record of the proceedings.

Plenary working has its limitations. A group of more than about ten is not usually a good setting for discussion. Not many people have the confidence to express their views freely in a large group. Only the more uninhibited participants are likely to tackle questions in any depth, and some may respond in more depth than you want them to! If you want everyone present to chip in their point of view and feel that it has been heard, it is as well to provide a smaller–scale working environment.

Also, communications can be surprisingly poor in plenary sessions. It is certainly not true that just because you have spoken to the whole group at once, everyone will have heard the same things being said. Misunderstandings are much harder to pick up and sort out in a large group. It is not unusual to find people with wildly different views and understandings of what has been happening.

Dividing up into smaller groups, you face an immediate choice. Will you have all the subgroups *working together in the same large room,* or will you try to find each group its own *separate working space?*

	All in Together	**Separate Rooms**
Advantages	Moving into groups and back into plenary is quick and easy. It is clear that everyone has been given the same information and asked to do the same things.	Groups are not distracted by half–overhearing other people's conversations. It is easier to build up a sense of trust and sharing within the group.
Disadvantages	Noise can be a serious problem — particularly if some members are hard of hearing. Groups have no privacy. People may be nervous of being overheard, or may be distracted by other groups' discussions.	Moving into groups and back into plenary is time–consuming and disruptive. Different groups may work in such different ways that they can't afterwards reach a common mind.

In general, when it is particularly important for everyone to cover the same ground, the all–in–together approach works better. It means that groups can tackle a number of different tasks and compare notes with each other as they go along.

Separate rooms come into their own when the groups are being asked to work independently on different parts of a common task; for example, a church conference looking at priorities for the next year might ask different groups to consider, say, finance, worship, social activities and education. When deep personal sharing is involved separate rooms are often more useful.

SETTING UP THE ROOM

Lecture Theatre

Setting the working area out in formal style, with rows of chairs and a table out front for the event leader, can be a good non–threatening way to start the proceedings, especially if most of the participants are not used to organized study activities. Nervous members can come early and get a good seat at the back. The lay-out gives people a comforting feeling that you are going to do all the work and they will just have to sit there and absorb your wisdom. Naturally you will not be letting them get away with that, but if you approach it sensitively, with a well thought out event design that catches their interest and puts them on familiar territory where they have a genuine contribution to make, they may never notice how much of the work they have done themselves!

The main drawback of lecture theatre style is that it doesn't lend itself to group discussion. In a setting this formal, people tend to address their remarks to the leader(s) rather than to each other, and the quieter–voiced find it difficult to make themselves heard.

Hollow Centred

Sitting everyone in a vast circle or horseshoe has the benefit that they can all see each other's faces, and makes it fairly easy to hear what is said. At least you can see who is speaking. Once the number in the circle goes beyond about twelve, though, the space in the middle starts to look big enough to make some people anxious. Often people cope with this by muttering comments to their neighbours rather than speaking out. The result can be a quite distracting level of noise. In large groups above twenty, it is probably better to accept this and build in plenty of deliberate requests for people to work together with their neighbours, rather than relying on straightforward plenary sessions.

Freeflow

This calls for light, easily movable chairs and plenty of space to put them in. Set up your working space with the chairs loosely grouped together. When you want the participants to work on an issue, ask them to join up with three or four other people sitting near them and cluster their chairs so that they can hear each other comfortably. When you want to bring them all together again, simply go to a suitable place where you won't have your back to anyone and call the group to order. Some small amount of chair–moving may be needed for everyone to see you, especially if you are using a flipchart, whiteboard, blackboard or overhead projector to record the working groups' results.

Once the small groups are established, you can flip backwards and forwards easily between working in clusters and working as a whole group. To make larger groups, simply ask each cluster to join with its neighbour.

Bistro Style

Set up your working space with small tables loosely grouped around a central focal point, each table surrounded by an appropriate number of chairs. The occupants of each table form a separate working group.

Bistro style is particularly useful where members of several different committees or interest groups meet to work on a common agenda. It has been used successfully at a conference of Church Councils from different churches in a neighbourhood. The table gives the group a clear visual focus. It is also a practical place to put any papers, drawings or other items in use.

Stuck in Pews

Fixed seating is not an utter disaster. Compact and effective working fours are easy. First ask everyone to join with the person next to them. Allow a few moments for "odd people" to sort themselves into pairs (the occasional three doesn't matter). Then ask each pair to join with the one behind or in front of them, again with a few moments to sort out partnerless pairs.

Once the fours have become established, it is usually possible to bring together two fours sitting next to each other as an effective working eight. Larger working groups don't often do well in fixed pews, because it is too difficult for people to see, hear and respond to each other.

The biggest problem with fixed pews usually comes when the groups report back. You can't pull up the pews into a more compact formation, so you face a choice whether to break up the working groups by asking everyone to move, or leave each group shouting its findings into echoing space. The kind of relaxed discussion between groups that comes naturally in freeflow and bistro style settings, is rarely possible under the curse of pews.

WHAT SIZE OF WORKING GROUP?

Pairs are the quickest and easiest to set up. Provided you (or another of the training team) are ready to count yourself in or out as necessary, you can divide any number into pairs.

Pairs are usually the best choice for straightforward sharing of personal opinions and stories. Two people can give each other a good hearing in far less time than a larger group requires. Besides being an economical use of time, pairs are usually not too threatening for those who are not confident, provided they don't find themselves partnered with someone unsympathetic.

Basic Pairs Exercise:

Ask each pair to decide who will speak first and who will listen first.

The speaker then gives his/her opinion or tells his/her story. The listener acts like a television interviewer, asking questions and prompting the speaker as necessary. When half the allotted time has gone by, the leader asks speaker and listener to swap roles.

Triads (groups of three) are more sophisticated than pairs, and a better choice for tasks that call for creative thinking. Triads are still small enough for good listening, but adding an extra member makes it easier for people to drop out of the conversation momentarily, reflect, then chip in from a fresh viewpoint.

Basic Triads Exercise:

Each triad chooses a speaker, a listener and an observer. Speaker and listener roles are the same as in the pairs exercise. The observers are asked to listen in silence and be ready to reflect back to the other two what they have observed. They may have a specific task (e.g. noting how easy the other two found it to listen to each other) or be left free to make more general observations. When the speakers have finished what they have to say, or when the leader calls time, the triads are then given a few minutes to hear the observer's reports.

Fours and Fives give a particularly useful size of small, lively working group. Any number larger than eleven can be divided exactly into a mixture of fours and fives. While these groups are really too big for effective personal sharing unless they are working in a private space with plenty of time available, they are excellent for other kinds of task. If the total number of participants is more than about forty, however, the time needed to collect together the working groups' findings may become a serious problem.

Six to Nine is getting rather large for less–confident participants to express their viewpoints easily, unless the group has private space, time and sensitivity enough to build up trust. If working groups this big are all in the same room, you will probably find it worth bullying them to move apart from each other and find their own working area, so far as space allows. It will be important to structure the group task with care. Concise, clear written instructions are useful. Any questions you want them to tackle should be kept as simple as possible and presented on paper, to avoid any confusion about exactly what is being asked. It is important to allow enough time for the group to get properly to grips with the task.

REPORTING BACK

The simplest kind of report back is where each group calls out its findings. If the information will be needed again later, one of the event leaders should be responsible for writing it up in clear, visible form.

The groups could be given a flipchart or large sheet of newsprint and invited to write up (or draw) what they want to put across, in their own style. The various sheets can then be displayed. One useful form of plenary is to give everyone a good slice of time, say over a coffee–break or meal, to move around and look at all the other groups' findings. Asking people to put a tick against anything they particularly like or agree with, a cross against anything they really don't go along with, adds a sense of how the participants feel as a whole.

On a gala occasion, the groups can really go to town on their reports with drama, people sculpture (on themselves or each other), artwork of any kind they like, a lecture with prepared overhead projector slides, etc.

Creative reflection on what has been said in the groups, in order to build up a shared understanding that takes account of everyone's insights, is part of the reporting–back process. If your team has the artistic skills, producing a large diagram or pictorial representation of the composite understanding you have reached can be a considerable help to people in taking it all in.

SERIOUS OCCASIONS

There are occasions in the life of any church which provide important opportunities for all the members to consider together, what belonging to that church means for them.

When the minister or vicar leaves, this is a useful point at which to:

- *look back* over the time spent together. What have been the memorable high spots; the comic disasters; the events that have become legends (*Do you remember that time when...*)? What changes have you seen together? Where are the areas of solid achievement? What strengths have you identified in your church, that you must now take care to maintain? Are there any areas of hurt or misunderstanding, that will need to be healed before you are able to put these years behind you?

- *celebrate* all that has been good about your time together;

- *take thought* for how the life of the church is growing and developing, and what that will call for in future; and in particular, what qualities you may want to look for in the next minister or vicar (if you have any choice in the matter!);

- *make arrangements* for managing the life of the church during the vacancy. Especially if the vacancy could be a long one, you will all need to think about how you will support those of your number who will carry the brunt of the extra work involved.

When a new minister or vicar arrives, that is a good opportunity to:

- *have a party* — show what kind of welcome your church can give.
- *introduce yourselves* and tell the new arrival as much as possible about the kind of church you are. This can be effectively done in a serious–jokey way such as asking everyone at the party to draw a coat–of–arms for your church showing the main features of church life, or write your entry in the "Good Churches Guide", or compose an estate–agent style blurb which might be used to sell people on the church's strengths and virtues.
- *let the newcomer introduce themself* in their own style: the style will probably tell you as much as the introduction!
- *sing, dance or otherwise make merry together.* Depending on your tastes this could mean a *Songs of Praise* type favourite hymns session, a barn dance, or getting the Youth Group to run a Golden Oldies Disco...

When you have a major evangelistic initiative planned, you need to:

- make sure *everyone understands what is planned,* and why;
- *train those with particular responsibilities* — doorstep visitors, or people giving public testimony, or members of a counselling team to work with enquirers;
- *help everyone think through* how they will support the initiative, practically, financially and above all by prayer; what it will mean for them if numbers of new people arrive in church; and how they can ensure a warm welcome.

EDUCATION WITHOUT CRUELTY

Learning occasions don't have to be serious and formal. Why not try breaking into a pizza–and–pasta evening, barn dance, faith supper or pie and peas night with a pub–style quiz? This could cover any area of knowledge you like. For example, a round of questions about the history of your own church; a round of Bible questions; an "acronyms round" asking people to give the full versions of such famous sets of initials as YMCA, SPCK, WARC, MAYC, JPIC, CCBI, QPS, BMS, GFS and PIM; a "Christians in the News" round; matching authors to well–known religious books, or singers to Gospel songs; a "Who are these people?" round with photographs; or "How well do you know the local community?"

An ecumenically–organized evening could be given added interest by asking each different church to contribute, say, one round of questions on their own tradition, two photographs, and two sets of initials to decipher.

It is important not to cram in too many questions, but to leave plenty of time for the teams to go through the answers together afterwards. Talking the answers over, particularly the ones they didn't know, can be a very effective way for people to take in new information. If you include a few questions of a more thought–provoking nature, surprisingly deep discussions can be touched off in a relaxed gathering of this kind.

Besides being fun in its own right, a well–handled quiz is an opportunity to raise the general level of interest in Church affairs, the Christian faith in general, or some particular issue. For most people, a quiz is non–threatening; it counts as "enjoyment" not "education". Nevertheless, it is a good way to find out how much you don't know. The very fact that it isn't taken too seriously can prompt people to go on and ask for real teaching on matters where a quiz has whetted their appetite.

Other painless learning possibilities include:

- *pilgrimages,* a long–standing tradition in the Christian Churches;
- *prayer vigils;*
- *social events with a serious theme,* such as hunger lunches;
- *processions* and other acts of public witness.

BIBLE STUDY

> *Those who accepted what he [Peter] said were baptized, and*
> *some three thousand were added to the number of believers*
> *that day. They met constantly to hear the apostles teach and*
> *to share the common life, to break bread, and to pray. A*
> *sense of awe was felt by everyone, and many portents and*
> *signs were brought about through the apostles. All the*
> *believers agreed to hold everything in common: they began*
> *to sell their property and possessions and distribute to every-*
> *one according to his need. One and all they kept up their*
> *daily attendance at the temple, and, breaking bread in their*
> *homes, they shared their meals with unaffected joy, as they*
> *praised God and enjoyed the favour of the whole people.*
> *And day by day the Lord added new converts to their num-*
> *ber.* (Acts 2.41–47)

1. Read the passage slowly aloud, several times. If you are studying it in a group, ask two or three different people to read it,
   maybe in different Bible versions, with a silent pause for reflection between the readings.

2. Start to pick out key words, phrases and images that particularly
   chime with the life of your own congregation. Speak these key
   words aloud, letting yourself see in your mind's eye the pictures
   of church life they conjure up for you.

   If you are in a group, explain to each other what your own particular key words mean for you. What words, phrases or images
   emerge as meaningful for the whole group? Write them on a
   large piece of paper. Can you see connections between them?
   You might find it helpful to draw lines in a different colour to
   indicate the connections.

   If you are working alone, take some blank postcards (or pieces
   of paper about postcard size). In the centre of each, write one of
   your key words/phrases. Taking each in turn, jot down around
   the central word the thoughts it suggests to you about church
   life. Now try to set out all the different cards in relation to each
   other. Do any obviously belong together? Are there any interesting disagreements?

3. Now read the passage again. How are you feeling your own
   church compares with the life of the early Church, as the writer
   of Acts describes it? Do you see any striking similarities? Any
   glaring differences?

4. Offer your findings to God in prayer. You may want to give thanks for particular joys and strengths in your church; express your sorrow at shortcomings or failures; ask for God's help in meeting particular needs, or finding the right way to respond to new opportunities.

5. Reflect prayerfully on how the learning activities you are involved with can best help your own church become a more faithful community of God's people. In what ways are you being freed to "sell all you have and share" each other's resources of knowledge, skill, insight and understanding?

IN-SERVICE DEVELOPMENT

Chapter Four tackles the whole area of in–service training for people with particular responsibilities in the church's life. It suggests some creative ways for experienced, competent church officers to reflect on their duties, as well as looking at skill enhancement and training for people taking on new responsibilities. Moving on to every–member ministry, how can lay church members and ordained clergy most fruitfully help each other's in–service development?

WHAT IS IT?

In–service Training (often called INSET) is something more and more Christians are becoming used to as a regular part of their working lives. Established managers put significant time and energy into studying management skills; trainers go on courses to enhance their training abilities; teachers are required to undertake regular professional development; large retailers provide structured training for their employees. In an increasing number of fields of work, lifelong professional learning is the expected norm rather than the exception.

Going on a training course doesn't mean you are bad at your work, or ignorant of how it should be done. Far from it. The enormous majority of INSET courses are enrichment opportunities for people who are already experienced, capable and doing a good job.

If you are looking for ways to develop new learning activities in your church, the idea of providing INSET for church officers frequently gets a warm welcome. People offering their time and talents to serve the church are often eager to do it better. Some may be sharply conscious of their own lack of training for what the church is asking them to do. Others may welcome a chance to chew over their working priorities together, or to look in depth at the ways in which their faith influences how they do their church job, and the effects that doing the job are having on their faith.

WHO NEEDS IT?

In the ideal situation, anyone taking on particular responsibilities within the life of the church would be expected to build in a regular time commitment for reviewing and reflecting on their work in company with others.

In the Church as in many other walks of life, the majority of serving officers are not new at their work. The guiding principle can seem to be "Why change a winning team?" This is often denounced as a bad thing: the same few faces going on year after year, with no new blood being brought in, and no scope for new people to be given responsibility. In a growing church, there are important questions to face about how, and how soon, new members can be given real tasks within church life.

The continuity has its positive side, though. When a person has put in the time, energy and commitment to become an effective Church servant, surely it is sensible stewardship of the Church's human resources to give them a fair stint in office.

Some experienced Church officers react indignantly to the suggestion of a chance to do in–service reflection. They seem to feel they are being insulted — told that they don't do their work well enough. There is an attitude of mind that says only novices need training.

There are two good reasons why that is a pity.

* *The world moves on* — there are often new skills and new insights that the most experienced officers have not yet come across.

* Acquiring new skills is only part, and not the most important part, of in–service development. Much more is about *deepening the spiritual base* from which people work, and that is a life-long task.

However, nobody needs training which ignores or rubbishes their existing expertise. If you work with adults who are experienced, capable and doing a good job, you must be seen to value the knowledge and skills they already have.

INDUCTION TRAINING AND INSET

Training of newly appointed church officers is often treated as a separate issue. The theory is that newcomers need to know all sorts of things that are old hat to established officers, and it would be really boring for the experienced people to have to sit through it all again.

The opposite approach is to involve experienced people directly in training the newly–appointed. This has a number of advantages.

• It can help ensure that the training offered meets the job's real practical needs.

• It offers first class refresher training for those drawn into the training team.

There's nothing quite like having to teach another person how to do your job, for making you look in depth at what you do, and how, and why.

Old hands and newcomers have a great deal to gain from working together on their common task of service. Old hands bring the insights of experience: knowing the task from the inside over a long period of time. Newcomers bring the insights of freshness: that particular sharpsightedness that you lose as soon as you know what is *supposed* to happen.

How much time should people be asked to give to training, alongside the time commitment they are making to the work itself? Obviously that depends on:

• *how much time they have* — people who are taking up some new responsibility because of a change in life that frees up their time, such as retirement, may be glad of the opportunity to spend time training with others;

• *how much is involved in the job.*

Where people are making a serious commitment that calls for extended training, there are three possible training models:

• *train them first,* then, perhaps after a commissioning service, let them start;

• *train them as they go along,* with weekly, fortnightly or even monthly sessions to take stock of what they are learning on the job, and teach them whatever else they need to know;

- *let them get to know the job first,* then after they've had a chance to get the feel of it, provide opportunities for training and reflection.

When you plan what you will offer your newcomers, consider building expectations about continuing development into their initial training.

LAY LEADERS

Different churches call out different kinds of servants (and give them different labels!).

- Some are chiefly concerned with *managing the church's affairs:* church council members, church secretaries, treasurers, clerks and administrators.

- Some centre their work on the *church building:* flower arrangers, banner makers, church cleaners, caretakers, vergers, gardeners, handymen (and women!).

- Some focus on *worship;* lay preachers, readers and service leaders, organists, guitarists, music directors, choir members and leaders, lesson readers and prayer leaders, drama or dance group members.

- Some have *education* as a main concern: Sunday school, youth group and housegroup leaders, bookstall managers, Lent group organizers, leaders of baptism, marriage, adult church membership or (in some traditions) confirmation preparation courses.

- Some are about *fellowship and outreach:* social organizers, sidesmen, befrienders, tea makers and washers–up, magazine editors and distributors, visitors and evangelists.

- Some are *pastoral:* lay counsellors and pastoral assistants, bereavement visitors, hospital and prison visitors.

- Some have a way of picking up a bit of most things: church wardens, church stewards, elders and deacons, sharing in the general oversight of the congregation, often find their duties developing new sides they never expected.

These are all prime candidates for in–service development.

Who are the regular servants of your church?

* Draw up a list of them. How is the church helping them to reflect on their calling and duties?

* When a person takes on some particular form of service in your church, is it clearly understood that they will also be expected to join INSET activities?

In–service programmes for leaders in the Church's educational work are particularly important. You need to model good practice. If you want everyone to believe you when you say in–service development is for everyone, you had better demonstrate how important it is to you by being seen to take your own INSET needs seriously.

Don't forget the clergy. Does your denomination provide INSET resources for its ordained ministers, and are your own clergy able to take full advantage of them?

Clergy sometimes find it difficult to take time out from their local responsibilities to attend training courses. If this is a problem for your clergy (your colleagues, if you are ordained), can they rely on your support and encouragement when training opportunities come their way? Does your learning strategy help everyone in the church see the value of giving clergy time to continue their ministerial education?

Are there any opportunities for involving clergy and lay people in reflecting together on the meaning of their responsibilities in church life — with somebody else leading the event? Clergy and lay people learning together demonstrates the important truth that *clergy are learners too.*

PLANNING YOUR INSET

When did you last review your church's INSET provision as a whole? Do any members of the congregation have professional experience that could be of help? For instance, you might find some members have been on good training courses themselves and brought back ideas, or even that you have people in the congregation with professional career development or training qualifications.

When you sit down to plan a piece of in–service training, it is important to *be clear what the main aims are*. Check through the list below adding your own ideas — and decide which aim is most important to you on this particular occasion.

1. *Fresh excitement*
   It can happen whether you've been serving for six months, or six years — or sixteen! You find yourself so wrapped up in doing your particular job that there is no time to remember why you wanted to do it in the first place. One good reason for in–service development is to put the fun back into serving.

2. *Your faith and this job*
   Taking on some particular church responsibility is bound to affect how you live your faith (less time for other things, to start with). It may bring you new insights, or challenge things you thought you were sure about. On the other hand, the way you do the job is shaped by your whole view of what being a Christian means. In–service development can be for reflecting on how to do your job in a more Christian way — as well as what the job is teaching you about being a Christian.

3. *New skills, techniques, strategies*
   We live in a world where new theories, new information and new technology move the goalposts every day. While St Paul pointed out the drawbacks of being "...tossed about by the waves and whirled around by every fresh gust of teaching..." (Ephesians 4.14), there are enough solid and valuable developments to ensure that people wanting worthwhile new ground to explore will rarely be disappointed. Besides issues directly concerned with your duties, it is worth considering more general topics such as time management, communication skills or team building.

4. *Seize a particular opportunity*
   For instance the chance of a session with an inspiring church leader, or some other famous and high-powered person. Church members and their relatives sometimes turn out to have hidden talents. If one member of a church team goes on a training event, church–organized or secular, they might be prepared to try leading something similar "back home". You could be offered the use of a training pack, or video, or spot a forthcoming television programme and decide to build something round that.

5. *Look at the biblical basis for your work*
    Whatever the work a person has taken on, there are important
    resources in the Bible for understanding it better.

6. *Review your working priorities*
    As everyone in ministry of any kind knows, there are always
    many more good and worthwhile things needing to be done
    than the time and other resources available can be stretched to
    fit in. Many church servants face difficult and painful choices
    between competing priorities — including family and work
    pressures.

7. *Deepen fellowship with colleagues*
    Fellowship activities are sometimes contrasted with training in
    rather a scornful way — "Oh, that was just a social occasion".
    Where your duties mean working as a team with other people,
    time spent getting to know and trust each other better is usual-
    ly time well spent.

8. *Study new developments in your area of responsibility*
    Changes in the law, new initiatives by your own denomina-
    tion, planning proposals in your local community, altered
    insurance company practice, even climate changes can make a
    big difference to a church servant's job... to say nothing of
    changes in the life of your own congregation.

9. *Consider how your work fits into the whole life of your church*

10. *Plan how to draw in new people to your area of work*
    Thinking about what kind of gifts and skills are needed for
    your job, how to attract people to it, how to choose and train
    them, can be a valuable exercise in itself.

The Diamond

If a group of you are working together, you might find this
exercise useful:

Write out a dozen or so different possible aims on pieces of
card. Now lay them out with: your *top priority* first; then
below it your *next two priorities* side by side; four *medium
priorities* across the centre of the diamond; two *low priorities*
below them; your *bottom priority* at the bottom. Anything
beyond these ten is *not a priority at all* on this occasion.

AN EVENING CONFERENCE FOR FLOWER ARRANGERS
(several different churches working together)

7.15 Participants arrive. Coffee and a chance to talk infor-
mally to one another. Maybe a display of books to
browse through at odd moments. Give each person a
sticky label and a choice of coloured pens. Ask them to
write their name on the label, and also draw a flower
that they are particularly fond of, then wear the label.

7.30 Introduction to the event. Practical notices (e.g. where
the toilets are). Tell the participants roughly what to
expect during the evening. Introduce the training team.

7.40 Ask participants to divide themselves up into groups of
about six and find a space for their group to work in,
pulling up their chairs so they can all hear each other
easily. When they are seated in groups, ask everyone to
introduce themself to their group, saying a bit about
who they are, where they come from and how long they
have been interested in flower arranging. Ask them also
to say what flower it is they have drawn on their name
label, and why they are fond of it.

7.50 Hand round to each group enough copies of the scribblesheet (see over) for everyone to have their own.
Encourage the groups to come up with as many
answers as possible to the question.

8.00 Ask them to look at their answers and decide which, for
them as a group, is the most important.

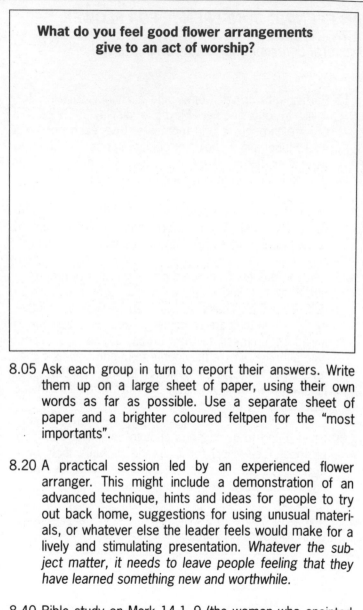

What do you feel good flower arrangements give to an act of worship?

8.05 Ask each group in turn to report their answers. Write them up on a large sheet of paper, using their own words as far as possible. Use a separate sheet of paper and a brighter coloured feltpen for the "most importants".

8.20 A practical session led by an experienced flower arranger. This might include a demonstration of an advanced technique, hints and ideas for people to try out back home, suggestions for using unusual materials, or whatever else the leader feels would make for a lively and stimulating presentation. *Whatever the subject matter, it needs to leave people feeling that they have learned something new and worthwhile.*

8.40 Bible study on Mark 14.1–9 (the woman who anointed Jesus).

Give each group enough copies of the Bible passage for everyone to have their own. Ask for a volunteer in each group to read the passage aloud. Invite all the participants to listen carefully, and underline or ring round anything in the passage that seems particularly to be saying something about their ministry as a flower arranger. After the groups have heard the passage, allow a few minutes of silence, then invite them to share with their fellow group members what words or phrases they have underlined, and why. What are they hearing in this word of Scripture?

8.55 A short guided meditation. This needs a leader accustomed to this kind of exercise, with previous experience of being led in meditation. Ask everyone to settle themselves in a comfortable, relaxed position and open with a brief relaxation exercise. Then guide them gently through the following meditation:

Imagine yourself in your own church. You are going to arrange the flowers for some particular occasion — any one you like — an important occasion, a humble occasion — you can choose... You can have whatever flowers you want... and whatever else you need... What flowers will you choose?... How will you arrange them?... Where in the church will they be?... Now it's done. You stand there and look at your work. How do you feel?... and as you stand there looking, you become aware that Jesus is standing right beside you, looking at your flowers... Does he speak to you?... Do you speak to him?... He touches one of the flowers... and smiles... and then, quietly, he leaves you. How do you feel now?

After the meditation, use a few simple words to bring people back to themselves. End with this or another suitable prayer:

Jesus, you are my Master and my Lord.
My whole life belongs to you.
My hands are yours.
My eyes are yours.
My heart is yours.
Fill my whole being with your love
*   so that in all of the things I make,*

> *the Father's glory may come shining through.*
> *In your dear name I ask it. Amen.*
>
> 9.10 A brief formal conclusion to the event, with thanks to
>   the leaders, the host church, and to the participants for
>   all that they have put into the evening.
>
>   It is good if there can then be coffee available again, so
>   that those people who don't have to rush off home
>   straight away can have a relaxed conversation with
>   each other, and, if a display of resource books has
>   been provided, another chance to browse. Be prepared
>   to throw them out with cheerful ruthlessness when it is
>   time to close up the building.

FORMING TRAINING GROUPS

Where people are undertaking lengthy training, it is a much richer
experience if they can share it in a group with others. You may be
lucky enough to be training a whole team of, for instance, lay
counsellors at the same time, so that they form a viable group on
their own. Fewer than four people don't really function as a group,
so a long–term training group needs at least six members, allowing
for people to be ill or have unbreakable rival commitments on
some occasions.

When people will be training together for a while, it is worth
taking care at the beginning to give them plenty of opportunity for
getting to know and trust one another, and at the end, to find a way
of celebrating all that the group has achieved together. One valuable way to organize the last session is a farewell party, at which
each person brings an item of food that says something about what
the course has meant to them; and the food is expounded before
being eaten. A shared act of worship makes the evening complete.

If you don't have enough people in training to form a viable
group by themselves, you'll need to explore the possibility of
involving people from other churches in your area. Working ecumenically isn't always appropriate, as every Christian tradition
organizes its lay leadership in its own way, and other circumstances vary too. It can be a very rich experience for an ecumenical group to reflect together on what they have in common; but
comparing unlike with unlike can also be highly frustrating.

However enormous your membership, it is worth not doing all your INSET inside your own church community: working with outsiders is a good protection against becoming in–bred and inward–looking. Inviting the neighbours in, or working with larger units of your own denomination, helps spread the benefit from all the time, effort and other resources put into developing training courses.

TIME AND BUSY PEOPLE

The traditional session times — evenings and weekends — are not always the most convenient. People may be tired after a long day, or giving up rare time with their family. For retired people evenings and weekends may be possible, but not their preferred times to be out. Why not have a preliminary training group meeting to brainstorm possibilities and decide which is most convenient? Breakfast time on Saturday, leaving the rest of the day free? Lunch time? The second half of a weekday morning? Sunday before or after normal morning or evening worship?

Residential training periods have powerful benefits; and equally powerful drawbacks. The experience of going away together, sharing meals, sleeping under the same roof, draws a group together as nothing else can. On the other hand, being away from home, especially at weekends, is difficult for many people. Friday suppertime to Saturday after lunch may be a possibility. The cost of residentials is greatly reduced if some of the group own touring caravans… Eating together, praying and worshipping together are possibilities even for groups who can't meet residentially.

GOING ON COURSES

If members of your education team have the chance to attend courses organized by your own denomination (or others) or a secular organization, discuss beforehand how you can maximize the knock–on effect afterwards. The same question may be worth asking if other church members go on courses.

TRAINING FOR SERVICE IN THE WORLD

Most of the lay ministry in your church will be offered, not by the few who take on particular tasks in church life, but by people whose main scope for Christian service and witness comes through their non–church activities (paid work, secular voluntary work, home–based caring and so forth). How does your church help them recognize what they are doing as part of their faith commitment, and grapple with the issues that raises for them?

Could you form "Practical Discipleship" groups to help people reflect together on their day–to–day ministries? This can be done either by bringing together people in similar lines of work, or by deliberately mixing the groups. Similar–interest groups will probably find it easier to talk about the detail of their work (though inter–agency rivalries could create problems, as could industrial secrets). Mixed interest groups could become a rich resource for exploring questions of shared concern — how you balance the demands of what your employer expects against the demands of pastoral confidentiality, for instance; or how you can *really* draw practical help from prayer when the heat is on.

Practical discipleship groups would be likely to find that giving each other prayer support became an important part of their task. If you could find ways for this to feed the main prayer life of the congregation (due confidentiality always being preserved), that in itself might open up resources for lay in–service reflection to people who couldn't spare the time to join any group.

If ordained ministers enjoy the opportunity to join with lay people whose main ministry is "detached" from the church set–up, both can benefit. The clergy can be much encouraged by finding out just how much good, solid, devoted service is being given all the time by people who make no fuss at all about it, indeed discount it as being "what anybody would do". The lay people can be equally encouraged by their clergy's reassurance that this is indeed acceptable Christian service. Both together can learn a great deal from thinking how their faith bears on all that they undertake.

BIBLE STUDY

> *There was at that time in Jerusalem a man called Simeon.*
> *This man was upright and devout, one who watched and*

waited for the restoration of Israel, and the Holy Spirit was
upon him. It had been revealed to him by the Holy Spirit that
he would not see death until he had seen the Lord's Messiah.
Guided by the Spirit he came into the temple; and when the
parents brought in the child Jesus to do for him what the law
required, he took him in his arms, praised God, and said:

"Now, Lord, you are releasing your servant in peace,
according to your promise.
For I have seen with my own eyes
the deliverance you have made ready
    in full view of all nations:
a light that will bring revelation to the Gentiles
and glory to your people Israel."

. . . There was also a prophetess, Anna the daughter of
Phanuel, of the tribe of Asher. She was a very old woman,
who had lived seven years with her husband after she was
first married, and then alone as a widow to the age of
eighty–four. She never left the temple, but worshipped night
and day with fasting and prayer. Coming up at that very
moment, she gave thanks to God; and she talked about the
child to all who were looking for the liberation of Jerusalem.
(Luke 2.25–32, 36–38)

1. Read the passage aloud. Do these two holy elders remind you of
   anybody you know? Think about your own years of service to
   the Church — long, short or just beginning. Who have been the
   people whose example has most inspired you? What was it
   about them, and their way of serving, that taught you most?

2. Simeon was *promised that he would not see death until he had*
   seen the Lord's Messiah. What do you particularly hope to see
   before your time of active service ends? Do you feel God has
   made you any promises about this? Have you made any promises to God?

3. Anna "never left the temple, but worshipped night and day with
   fasting and prayer." How do you feel about that as a model of
   Christian service? Do you think there's a real chance that in
   your own church, the faithful handful will become so bound up
   in church duties that they have no time for other kinds of activity? If so, how much does it matter? Who pays the price?

How about someone like Anna, with no "home responsibilities"?

4. What is the age balance like among your serving lay officers?
Does your church seem to find it easiest trusting young, middle–aged, or retired people? What does this reflect about your
life together as a church? How do you value each of the age
groups and give them a true sense of belonging? How do you
honour the people who, for whatever reason, are past active service? What ministries does your church accept from aged, frail,
physically impaired and/or housebound people?

5. Read the passage again. What do Simeon and Anna have to
teach you about the nature and purpose of in–service development for Christian ministers, lay or ordained? If you have the
chance, you might try working on this with clay. Take a
good–sized lump of clay and knead it in your hands, reflecting
on the passage of Scripture and all it is teaching you about
in–service development. Don't start by trying to model anything in particular: just work the clay until you see what it
wants to turn into. If you're doing this as one of a group, allow
plenty of time to look at what you have produced and reflect on
each other's work. You can learn a great deal from discussing
what each of you has made, and why, and also what the other
group members see in it.

LEARNING THROUGH WORSHIP

Chapter Five looks at worship, and in particular the sermon, as a channel for adult Christian education. How satisfactory is it to treat the sermon as a learning tool? How do you tie preaching in with other educational activities? What alternatives are there to the traditional sermon?

A crucial part of adult Christian learning comes through practising our faith in prayer, worship and Bible study. The public worship we join in weekly, shapes our understanding of who God is and what he wants from us.

For new Christians, worship sometimes takes a bit of getting used to: when to sit and when to stand, for instance. How does your church help newcomers to know what is expected of them?

- Are there any limits on *where people can sit,* and if so, are they really necessary? How do you prevent embarrassing misunderstandings? History abounds with horror stories of people whose experiences in church taught them only that they didn't seem welcome to sit *anywhere.*

- If you use *books* in worship, are they easy to find your way around? Do people unfamiliar with the words find themselves squinting painfully at microscopic print? If there is a written order of service, do you as a matter of course tell people where you've got to, at regular intervals? Do you use a single hymn book, or expect people with the normal number of arms to juggle three books and a handful of loose leaflets?

- What kind of *language* do you use in prayers, hymns, sermons, and when the worship leader addresses the congregation? (This is a more complicated issue than it seems; in a congregation that always uses straightforward, easily understood modern language, some new Christians may hanker after the church they knew as children, or the church they always imagined, and yearn for the majestic prose of bygone ages.) How do you help new members to become familiar with Christian jargon — "salvation", "repentance", "grace", "sin", "eternity", "cleansing and renewal" and so forth? Are you entirely certain that even the established members of the church know what it all means?

- How do you as a church react to *"mistakes"* in worship — people sitting when they should be standing, or being in the wrong place at the wrong time, or getting the words wrong? Do you stiffen or titter, or say something kindly meant to put the person straight, or even quietly join them in doing it their way? One of the many gifts mentally handicapped people can give to a congregation able to accept them as full members, is helping everyone to be much more relaxed and joyful about unexpected things that happen during worship . . .

Your scope for influencing the ways your church learns through worship will depend on your personal role. If you are the duly ordained minister in pastoral charge, you will be able to do a good deal on your own authority. If you are a humble member of the congregation working on delegated authority from the clergy or church council, you'll have to go through the proper channels. If you have no formal authority at all, but only the sense that God is asking you to be concerned for adult learning in your church, you can always try persuasion.

Always bear in mind that nobody, not the most autocratic, "Father–knows–best" of vicars, not the most illuminated of Spirit–driven charismatic leaders, owns the Church's worship as private property. What you can do is limited both by the rules of your denomination (if you belong to one), and by the consent of the congregation.

LEARNING FROM THE BUILDING

If you look around your church building, you will probably find various features which help make it a stimulating learning environment. There may be stained–glass windows showing biblical scenes or events. There may be carvings, painted panelling, murals. In many traditions there will be large representations of the Cross. Special trouble may have been taken to surround the altar or holy table with depictions of Christ's Passion. All of these are useful resources, but some may be more obviously self–explanatory than others. Interpreting the less familiar pictures and symbols can be a revelation not only to newcomers, but also to people who have seen them so often they hardly notice them any more, yet have never really known what they mean.

The design of the building directs people's attention to where particularly significant things happen. In some traditions the eye is gathered to where Holy Communion is celebrated. In others, pride of place goes to the pulpit where the Word is preached. A prominent font or baptistery may call to mind the sacrament of baptism; there may be a place of honour for the reading of Scripture. The architecture as a whole may function to create space, awe, a sense of mystery and upward movement; or comfort and homeliness; or an atmosphere of great historical continuity.

If you don't worship in a purpose–made church building, either because you don't have one or as a matter of Christian principle, it is still worth thinking about the strengths of the building you *do* worship in. What kind of atmosphere does it have? What are its distinctive features? How much scope do you have for changing it, moving the fixtures and fittings around, altering the decoration?

Your church council, education committee, worship committee, ministry team or other responsible body might usefully check up from time to time on how effectively your regular worship exploits the natural strengths and advantages of your building. Are there any particular drawbacks and disadvantages to be overcome?

You can make your church a more stimulating place to worship by putting eye–catching *visual material* in prominent places. This technique has a long history.

- The *icons* which feature so prominently in Orthodox worship, and are sometimes now found in churches of other traditions, serve as a devotional focus. Lighting candles in front of them symbolizes the believer's prayer, offered to God through meditation on the icon. Christians from Reformed traditions can be deeply uneasy about anything that smacks of image–worship; but can also gain a great deal from learning to use icons the way Orthodox Christians do, finding out how and why they are painted, and what all the features signify.

- Many churches use *banners* to feed eye and mind. Making banners, putting together word and image, is a valuable way of helping people to develop new theological insights.

- *Paintings* of many kinds have their place in worship. Not only beautiful landscapes and scenes from Scripture: urban desolation matters to God too. Religious art can raise questions about what images are appropriate for the Church in our day. For instance, in the multi–racial nation that is modern Britain, and the many–coloured community that is today's Christian Church worldwide, what does it say if Jesus is always shown as pink–cheeked and blond?

LEARNING THROUGH PRAYER

The words we use in worship have a powerful influence on our faith. The familiar words of the Lord's Prayer and Grace, which new Christians may well know already from school assemblies or *Songs of Praise,* sink deep into our understanding, gaining new meanings as we ourselves grow and are changed.

Just saying the Lord's Prayer carefully and reverently, listening to the meaning of the words as you say them, can be a highly fruitful learning experience. Christians who form the habit of saying the same prayer(s) daily, embed the words they use at a level of consciousness where they work profoundly on the whole understanding. In the Orthodox tradition, praying the Jesus Prayer ("Lord Jesus Christ, have mercy on me") can become a lifetime's vocation.[1] Some Catholic Christians use the Rosary as a daily prayer discipline.[2] Christians involved in justice and peace work might join in praying the Universal Prayer for Peace at noon each day.

The Anglican and Roman Catholic daily Offices of Morning and Evening Prayer are a more complex exercise: a meditation on the Psalms and on daily reflections from Scripture, in the light of canticles of praise from Old and New Testaments.

Many Christians, of all traditions, have their own simple pattern of daily prayer working quietly away at the shaping of their faith.

Why not offer a session or two on *"Prayer in Daily Life"* and see if you can find any takers?

You might try a series of events at different times of day, targeting different groups of people. For example, a weekday afternoon session aimed at retired people; a late morning session with toddler activities alongside, for parents with young children at home; a midweek evening session for people who are at work during the day; a Sunday evening session (after evening worship, maybe?) for people who are too busy during the week.

Keep these first sessions simple: a chance for people to compare experiences and raise whatever issues are of most concern to them, plus something more adventurous from the leader. This might be teaching them a new prayer technique, offering some ideas about places to pray, an exercise on spirituality and personality types, or what you will.

If the session goes well, people might ask for more. Two particularly good resources for running a longer course on prayer are *Helpful Habits* by Graham Pigott (Grove Spirituality Booklets no. 31) and the video *Seven Circles of Prayer* (Housetop Communications).

PRAYER IN PUBLIC WORSHIP

The prayers people join in during public worship, either by speaking them along with the worship leader or by listening and saying "Amen", frequently bring new insights to challenge and extend their understanding of faith. Striking a liberating vein of prayer that fires people up with true vision carries greater rewards than any other learning method available.

There are, however, strict limits on the deliberate use of prayer for learning purposes. When you lead a congregation's prayer, by creating a prayer in your own words, or using words others have written, or presenting words to be spoken together, you are offering people expressions for their own reaching–out to God. Being offered the right words to express the prayer in your heart is a wonderful learning experience. Being forced to join in a prayer that sets your hair on end ("I can't say Amen to *that!*") is probably also a learning experience, but a deeply disturbing one.

You "put words into people's mouths" in a particularly intimate way when you ask them to join in saying a piece of liturgy. While in theological terms saying "Amen" undoubtedly betokens as absolute a consent as speaking the words yourself, there is something about fitting your own tongue round a prayer somebody else has written — especially if you are new to all this, or come from a tradition where, the Lord's Prayer excepted, it is not normal custom. For this reason, although there are huge quantities of excellent prayers in print, ancient and modern, formal and informal, radical and conservative, sober and exuberant, choosing whether, when and how to include them in your congregation's worship is a matter for care and discernment.

(Wo)Man from Mars

One Sunday when you don't have to be out at the front leading (if you genuinely *never* have a Sunday like that, ask a lay
member of your education team to do the exercise for you),
find an inconspicuous place to sit. During the service, try to
listen to the prayers offered as if you were a visitor from
outer space, that is, as if you were hearing it all for the first
time.

What ideas about God come across to you from the prayers
used? What does God seem to be like, and to be interested
in? What is God pleased by? offended by? What does "obeying
God" appear to mean in practice?

Unless your memory is razor sharp, you will find it useful to
keep brief notes of what you hear. Do this inconspicuously,
on the back of the notice sheet or maybe in a very small
notebook — you don't want people to be distracted from
their worship by wondering what you're up to.

Chewing the results over, preferably with others, afterwards,
should tell you a great deal about learning needs, opportunities and existing good fruits in this part of your church's worship.

Intercessions can widen our view of God's concern for his world
and its inhabitants. Who gets prayed for in your church, and how
are their needs introduced to the congregation? What line do you
take on "including the notices in the intercessions" by adding a
word of explanation as part of each bidding? Do you ever link
prayers for some particular need with a display of information
about it, say in the fellowship area (see p. 26)?

What view of *lay discipleship* do your intercessions put forward? Do you pray for people in their secular calling, or only for
the things they do "on the church's headed notepaper"?

What *political understandings* do your prayers carry? Do you
pray for, say, joy–riding urban youngsters as wrongdoers in need
of repentance; as victims in need of rescue; as manifestations of a
sick society in need of healing; or as beloved children of God in
need of affirmation? How do you pray for South Africa, in a congregation where some leading members, perhaps with family in

South Africa, see the African National Congress as God's agents keeping alive the hope of a just settlement; and others, perhaps also with family in South Africa, see them as one–settler–one–bullet terrorists? How do you pray about AIDS? What help can you give people, when exploring the issues involved, both through the way you phrase your prayers and outside the service?

HYMNS

Hymns are another well–established traditional tool for teaching theology to the faithful. A careful choice of hymns adds enormously to the learning impact of a service. *Mission Praise* and its successors have done a great deal to spread the use of good, lively new hymns and praise songs, even among more cautious congregations.

Because people are often less wary about the theology of what they sing than what they pray, hymns can be a highly promising way to introduce new viewpoints and new insights into your worship. Unfamiliar words can be wed to familiar tunes. If you choose your tune carefully, so that the "usual words" are ones which complement and enhance the new ones, the effect can be very rich with meaning. For example, singing Brian Wren's beautiful Calvary hymn "Here hangs a man discarded" to the Passion Chorale, "O sacred Head sore wounded".

In recent years, hymns from other Christian cultures in different parts of the world have been brought into use in Britain, through the mission and aid agencies, the Iona Community, the international ecumenical movements and other forms of direct personal contact. Adding them to your church's repertoire is a powerful way of sharing what it means to be part of the World Church: "a vast throng, which no one could count, from all races and tribes, nations and languages, standing before the throne and the Lamb." (Revelation 7.9)

LITURGY ON SPECIAL OCCASIONS

Every church has its special occasions. Besides the great festivals of Christmas and Easter, there are:

- other *feasts of the Christian year* — more or fewer of these according to your tradition!;

- *community festivals* such as Harvest and Remembrance Day;

- *family celebrations* around welcoming the newly born, receiving new people into church membership, marriages and funerals;

- *local church occasions:* dedication festivals, chapel or church anniversaries, patronal feasts, flower festivals, centenary celebrations, etc;

- *local community occasions* such as Show Sunday services, civic services, parade Sundays for uniformed youth organizations, and special acts of worship for needs in the community — like the prayer vigils offered in many churches during the Gulf War, particularly in places where local young people were involved in the fighting;

- *ecumenical occasions* such as Women's World Day of Prayer, the Week of Prayer for Christian Unity, Christian Aid Week, One World Week and the United Nations Day of Prayer for World Peace.

All of these offer possibilities for something that bit extra in the way of liturgy. Your church's taste may run to an incandescence of candles, clouds of incense and sumptuous vestments on everyone down to the doorkeeper; or barbed wire wreathing the pulpit, songs of protest and liberation on the organ and liturgical drama all down the aisles; or glories of extempore prayer and an extra–long sermon; or belting out your favourite hymns in four–part harmony; or praising the Lord with a loud voice on guitars, recorders, tambourine, trumpet, lyre and synthesizers; or an hour of extra–deep and pregnant shared silence. What matters is to find the right way of being yourselves, offering that occasion, in the presence of the Lord of glory.

The next chapter looks in more detail at the whole issue of special occasions in the Church's life as an opportunity for learning together.

THE SERMON

You sometimes hear clergy say, "The Sunday sermon is the only adult Christian education my people ever get." It will be obvious by now that this book takes a different view. Nevertheless it probably *is* true to say that preaching in worship gives many people the only *organized* adult Christian education they get.

Adult Educators and Preachers

All preachers have a claim to be called adult educators, but not all adult educators are licensed to preach. If you're a lay person with no preaching ministry yourself, how do you go about tying in sermons with other educational activities?

As a non–preacher, your scope for negotiating linkages will depend crucially on building up the right kind of relationship between adult education team and preaching team. A good two–way relationship between adult educators and preachers can be fruitful in many ways. It makes the preachers more sensitive to their educational responsibilities, and the educators more aware of their work's theological implications. It helps keep the educational work firmly in the mainstream of church life, and the preaching well–informed about the needs, hopes and aspirations of the membership. Preachers may become adept at picking things up from learning exercises and developing them into sermons. The educators might even become adept at picking things up from sermons and developing them into learning exercises.

If you are a preacher, or indeed the only preacher in your church, then unless you're a total one (wo)man band you'll still find it worthwhile to build up good two–way relationships between your preaching role and those engaged in adult education leadership. You might consider occasionally inviting one of the education team to give an address, or take up one of the suggestions on page 75 about sermon alternatives.

Another possibility is *sermon preparation groups*. If you are planning a learning initiative and a sermon series in parallel, try asking some of the team to meet with you early in the week and help you prepare your sermon for the next Sunday. Chewing over the Bible passages together can throw rich shafts of new light, and the discussion may considerably improve both sermon and learning venture.

The Sermon as a Learning Opportunity

You will have your own views about how far it is satisfactory to treat the sermon as a learning tool. At one extreme, some preachers feel they are only empowered to offer the pure Word of God, with no interference from outside concerns. At the other extreme, some preachers feel all that really matters is telling the congregation what they need to hear on that particular occasion. Most of us come somewhere in between.

There are, of course, many different kinds of sermon. Some preachers distinguish between inspirational and teaching sermons; or between teaching and prophetic. All of these should involve the congregation in learning of different kinds. The sermon that lights no new candles in people's hearts is a wasted opportunity — "for the kingdom of God is not a matter of words, but of power." (1 Cor 4.20).

Children's addresses, or sermons preached in an all–age setting, offer particular opportunities. You can explain complex truths in simple language; you can quote passages from fantasy fiction; you can invite audience participation; you can ask people to look at pictures, make paper aeroplanes to illustrate riding on the breath of the Spirit, even *talk to their neighbours;* and nobody will resent it because the children are there to give you all an alibi!

Where your intention as a preacher is to provide people with new information, what kinds of information do you feel happy providing? What view do you present of the nature of the biblical text, and what kind of evidence do you bring in support of that view? Should modern critical principles of Biblical exegesis get into sermons? How much of the scholarly and critical scaffolding supporting your interpretation should be left on view in the finished sermon?

What ought your sermons to do to people's concepts of faith? Should you:

- *collude?* Ought everything you say to be in line with what you think the congregation believes?

- *affirm?* Do you need to make it clear that you value their faith, and want to help them be confident about its strengths?

- *expand?* Is it your task to explore wider possibilities, to push back the frontiers of their, and your own, vision?

- *challenge?* Do they, and you, need to look seriously at the ways in which your present grasp of faith is incomplete, and be ready to move on?

- *confront?* Should you tell them when, in conscience, you are convinced that they are wrong?

- *undermine?* Given the command to be "wary as serpents" as well as "innocent as doves" (Matthew 10.16), where you find yourself in disagreement with (some of) your congregation about the nature of faith, is there something to be said for the subtle approach? How will you respond if people tell you that your preaching has caused their faith to collapse from under them?

Would you give the same answer every week, or do you find that different circumstances demand different priorities?

Where you deliver a sermon, or series of sermons, intended to teach people about some area of faith, could there be a case for using OHP slides (see p. 30) to illustrate the points you are making? How about giving lively, well–produced handouts for people to take away and think about during the week?

Teaching sermons don't have to be a matter of telling people things. The educationalist Paulo Freire developed a technique he called *problematizing* for bringing people to grips with an issue by presenting it to them in the form of a question or problem, rather than providing answers. This bears a striking resemblance to Jesus' practice of teaching by parables, puzzles that his hearers carried away with them to work at in their own lives. Prompting people to do their own thinking will only work if you ask your questions in a way they can relate to, and consider critically in the light of their own knowledge and experience. For example, a sermon on "Living your life in the expectation of Jesus' second coming" might begin by asking people how they would behave if they knew somebody really important was coming to stay with them next week.

Linking Sermons with Educational Initiatives

When your church is putting time and energy into a major learning venture, you will probably want to link it up in some way with the sermon at the main weekly service(s). The preacher(s) will need to be fully briefed about:

- the nature and purpose of the adult learning venture

- the nature of the link between sermon and event — a sermon about the event; on the event theme, or some particular part of it; on a text that will be key to the event?

If it is difficult to justify giving main service time to something which perhaps only involves a few people, smaller services (evening or midweek, if you have them) could be the place to preach the link sermon.

Sermons often form part of a weekend away, or other training event, and if so, will need marrying in with the rest of what is planned. If practically possible, the preacher(s) should attend at least some of the event planning meetings, to be clear about what the event organizers have in mind. Whether full planning team membership is appropriate depends on the preacher's personal interests, skills and time priorities.

Creative writing exercises which invite people to produce their own poems, prayers, hymns or meditations, may produce rich resources for incorporating into the next week's sermon, or indeed for longer–term use.

Besides linking sermons to educational activities, a learning church calls for preaching built around the same vision as the learning programme. Anchored in the whole mission of the church and taking people's secular vocations seriously, sermons need to explore lay discipleship and lay dilemmas. The facts of faith relate to the everyday universe, made by God, loved by God and kept by God; for we share "[the hope] that the universe itself is to be freed from the shackles of mortality and is to enter upon the glorious liberty of the children of God." (Romans 8.21) Sermons are about nothing if not real life.

Linking Educational Initiatives with Sermons

If your church follows a lectionary, the weekly lessons can also guide housegroup, Bible study group or all–age learning sessions. In the same way, a major sermon series can easily be tied to other learning activities.

Some churches use a Sunday pattern of a quiet, reflective ser‑ vice; then an hour or so of Christian learning around the week's Bible lessons for all ages, either separately in groups or working together; then an exuberant family service. People attend the learning session plus one (or both) of the services.

In churches that are happy to experiment with forms of worship, you might develop new pieces of Bible–based worship alongside the preaching. This might involve creating drama, dance, litanies, hymns, meditations or more extended acts of worship.

Alternatives to the Sermon

If the congregation will consent to it, there are many rewarding alternatives to the traditional sermon.

* *Pulpit dialogues* — two preachers discuss the text or theme together.

* *Group sermons* — a group of people prepare a sermon together, or each offer their own linked reflections on the text.

* *Audiovisuals* — a suitable tape–slide presentation, say, or a meditation built around pictures on photographic or OHP slides.

* *Favourite hymns* — one or more members of the congregation choose a hymn and say why it is important to them; one of the preaching team might then add further thoughts about it.

* *Iconic meditations* — copies of an evocative picture are distributed among the congregation, and a speaker guides them in reflecting on it.

* *Dramatic sketches* — Riding Lights, the Iona Community and others publish excellent books of short playscripts. Dramatized *readings from Scripture* are another possibility.

* *Listening to music* can be well–received *if* you manage to choose a piece that suits everyone's taste. Performances from *music and singing groups* may give young people a chance to make an appreciated contribution.

Breaking people into discussion groups during sermon time can cause real discomfort for people who hate being made to switch into "intellectual mode" when they are trying to worship. On the plus side, a well–designed question can spark off really fruitful joint exploration in churches that don't mind giving it a try.

Because evening worship often has a quieter and more contemplative atmosphere, the Sunday evening sermon slot may be a specially appropriate place to try some of the quieter alternatives:

- contemplative exercises;
- guided meditations;
- shared silence.

Midweek services, if you have them, can offer similar opportunities.

BIBLE STUDY

So the Speaker, in his wisdom, continued to instruct the people. He turned over many maxims in his mind and sought how best to set them out. He chose his words to give pleasure, but what he wrote was straight truth. The sayings of the wise are sharp as goads, like nails driven home; they guide the assembled people, for they come from one shepherd. (Ecclesiastes 12.9–11)

1. What are sermons for? What are you doing when you preach? Sometimes it is like holding a jewel of familiar Scripture and turning it until the light catches it just *so*, to reveal the fire hidden at its heart. Sometimes it is more like bringing in treasures found on the beach — this thought–provoking conversation overheard in the pub; that newspaper article; the other insight sparked off by the words of a pop–song or a poster seen in the street. Sometimes it is like dropping depth–charges: the parable, the poem, the haunting word–picture that stays in the hearer's imagination a long while, sparking off learning at many levels. What are *your* favourite metaphors for preaching?

2. Preparing a sermon is a powerful learning experience for the preacher. There's something about paying close, detailed attention to the word of Scripture in order to discern what it's saying for the present moment in time and place. It changes you — far more, I suspect, than hearing the sermon ever changes your congregation. What do you think is happening when a preacher "turns over many maxims in his (or her) mind and seeks how best to set them out"? What, for you, are the most important aspects of sermon preparation?

3. "He chose his words to give pleasure, but what he wrote was straight truth." Does that spark anything off for you, about the practical dilemmas preaching involves?

4. "The sayings of the wise are sharp as goads, like nails driven home; they guide the assembled people, for they come from one shepherd." End your study with a time of shared prayer. You may want to: give thanks for all that your church gains through worship; pray for your preachers, that the "one shepherd" may guide them in wisdom. You could finish by reading the text aloud together.

Notes

1 See *The Way of a Pilgrim,* trans. R A French (Triangle, 1986).

2 See for instance, *How to Pray the Rosary,* Sister Mary Francis (Mayhew–McCrimmon, 1975).

FEASTS, FASTS, AND FESTIVALS

Chapter Six presents some ideas for building learning opportunities around special festivities. Besides the major feasts of the Christian year it includes celebrations in the life of the local church, community and family occasions. It also reviews the scope for educational activities during seasons of preparation for festivals.

People with the Holiday Spirit Will Do Things they'd Never Dream of Trying in "Real Life".

The "holiday factor" can spice up the learning life of your church:

- Have you come across some *gala educational exercise* you would really like to give people the chance of experiencing? Why not save it for the next suitable festivity and make it an occasion to remember?

- Celebrating a festival is something even *busy people* will make time for. Take a look at any special occasions your church will be celebrating in the next year and see if they offer opportunities for lively adult learning.

- *How your church celebrates festivals* says a lot about the kind of faith you have. If people come in to join your worship at a festival time, what messages are they getting? Why not bring a group together to think about it and maybe suggest some changes? Try starting off with:

Guided Meditation

You have never been to church before.

Take a moment to decide what sort of person you are: how old, tall, slim or well padded? Well-to-do or hard-up? What clothes have you put on, to go to church in?

There is to be a special service at the church today — what is it? A feast day in the Church year, a flower festival, a family wedding — what?

Are you going alone or with others?

Just before you leave home to set out for church, you look at yourself in the mirror. How do you feel?

Now you are on your way. Do you have far to go? Walking, bus, car...?

You're outside the church building, looking at it. What sort of building is it — how big, how old, what style? Where do you have to go to get inside? Is it easy to see that you've come to the right place?

You walk to the door and go inside. What do you see? What happens next?

After the meditation, give people plenty of time working with a partner to talk over what they "saw" and how they felt about it. When they've had a good long chance to work it through, ask them to share with the whole group any ideas that come to them for improving the way your church celebrates on festival occasions.

Does your church believe in parties? Jesus was gossiped about for enjoying himself too much (Matthew 11.18–19, Luke 7.33–35) — *are you*??

CHRISTIAN FEASTS

Over the last ten years or so, Christians of all traditions have been rediscovering *Holy Week* and *Easter* as powerful opportunities for learning and sharing together — and for reaching non–Christians with Good News.

Studying the Passion Gospel together is something Christians have been learning from for nearly two thousand years.

- Simplest can be most effective: meeting to hear the Gospel read aloud, then offering people a chance to share together what the text has said to them. Everybody knows the Easter story, but how often do we *really* listen to the words? And each of the four Evangelists tells it his own distinctive way.

- Having different people read the different parts, with one person to be narrator, opens new facets. Everybody brings their own particular understanding to it; reading a part, even if it is only the crowd shouting "Crucify him!", can take you inside the text in new and unexpected ways. Active Gospel readings help bring Easter worship alive. For even more effective learning, make sure people later have a chance to take stock together of all that has struck them as they read and/or listen.

- Why not a Passion pilgrimage, maybe through your city/town/village centre? You need to find the places in your own community that match the scenes of Jesus' passion: a parsonage or manse for the house of Caiaphas, a central church hall for the trial before the Sanhedrin, maybe outside the town hall or council offices for the trial by Pilate. Either use the traditional Stations of the Cross or go back to the book and develop your own. Could you do it ecumenically? Can you carry a cross, preferably a big, heavy one made of well–used timber? Perhaps you could carry other symbols as well, such as a candle wreathed in barbed wire to honour today's prisoners of conscience? Or design and make your own banners: what images do the anointing at Bethany, the cleansing of the Temple, the Last Supper, Jesus' ordeal in the garden, the trial before Pilate and all the rest spark off for *you*? Children and young people can be brilliant at this — especially if adults work (sensitively) with them.

- Some churches have experimented with a "Way of the Resurrection" along the same lines, presenting the events of Easter Morning and the Risen Lord's appearances to the disciples. If you fancy trying something similar, why not begin with a Lent project working out which scenes should be included and how they can be presented in modern terms? David Jenkins, the Bishop of Durham has made the Resurrection front–page news several times in recent years. So what do *you* believe about the Resurrection — and how might you put that over, to fellow–Christians or, if you feel brave, to the general public?

The traditional *Easter liturgies* offer enormously rich resources for learning through worship. This is true whether your church prefers to use the complete service as set, or is happy to pick and adapt.

- One piece of Easter liturgy carefully placed in an otherwise "free" service can be deeply moving. So can building something spontaneous into an otherwise formal service; or a time of shared silence, perhaps with an evocative photographic slide projected on to a large screen at the front of the worship area; or ask one of your best flower–arrangers to create something.

- A "Christian Passover" service during Holy Week can be a tremendous revelation of the spiritual power of our Jewish roots.

- On Maundy Thursday evening, commemorating our Lord's last supper with his disciples offers a moving reminder of all that Jesus gave up for our sake. Footwashing, though it troubles some Christians by its intimacy and others by putting the minister in the role of Christ, can also be a humbling experience of our oneness with those first disciples — in all their confusion and sometimes wrongheadedness, as well as in the joy of the Lord's presence. Keeping vigil after the service, in remembrance of Jesus' lonely agony in Gethsemane, is an opportunity for deep reflection on his sufferings.

- Many Christian traditions are re-discovering an ancient custom in their Good Friday worship, which began in Jerusalem in the second or third centuries, of focusing on a cross. Some Christians, following the Taizé custom, gather together and kneel (or sometimes prostrate themselves) around a simple cross, with a mixture of silence, reading and songs. Others, particularly from the Catholic and Orthodox traditions, venerate the cross by either touching it or kissing the feet of the image of the crucified. This could be a practical way to express reverence which might be appreciated by many, not least children, God made us as embodied creatures, and using our bodies in acts of worship often sparks fresh levels of understanding.

- Dawn services on the hills (sometimes in snow!) can bring Christians of different traditions out to share an act of worship before the day's main celebrations begin. If the service includes simply breaking bread together with no attempt at copying a full Eucharist, it can make even Christians from traditions that do not use sacraments feel at home, as well as avoiding problems around impaired communion.

Adopting something new into your Easter worship could inspire a learning exercise to help people reflect on what they will be doing, and maybe deepen their whole worship experience. Beware of making vast changes in the main service, though. People often feel robbed if an act of worship they have known and loved for many years becomes unrecognizable, or if they think their denominational loyalty is being undermined.

Christmas creates a unique chance of getting people's attention, inside *and* outside the Church, to think about who Jesus is for us today. Each year there is careful and creative media work about the true meaning of Christmas, alongside all the gruesome gluttony and rampant consumerism.

Reclaiming Christmas as the celebration of Jesus' birthday has made a great deal of progress in recent years.

• Ventures such as "Christmas Unwrapped" and "Christmas Cracker" provide ideas, resources and training opportunities for churches concerned to witness to the true Christian feast against usurpation by Yuletide over–indulgence.

• Churches near shopping centres often find it rewarding to keep their church buildings open, with chaplains (lay as well as ordained) in attendance both for security reasons and to be available if people come wanting a listening ear. The Christmas pressure to "be with the family" creates great misery for some whose family will not be with them, or whose family relationships are unhappy. It is important to prepare the chaplains for coping with whoever may walk in, and give guidance on how to handle situations they are not equipped to deal with by themselves.

• Where churches make a special effort to give Christmas hospitality, to people living alone, or to mentally handicapped people living "in the community", or to students spending Christmas far from home, the hosts may find themselves unexpectedly learning a great deal — and not only how other people, or peoples, celebrate Christmas. "Crisis at Christmas" ventures providing homeless people with Christmas shelter and food can also be powerful learning experiences. If your church undertakes anything like this, why not build in an Epiphany party where people can talk over with each other how it all went?

• The idea of "birthday presents for Jesus" could be a useful base for all-age learning activities during the lead–up to Christmas. Pairing one adult with one child is often a very creative combination; the children can surprise the adults by their insight into the meaning of Christmas, and sometimes the adults also surprise the children by their youngheartedness. The results might be a banner, a mural, a huge Christmas presents mobile, a scatter of practical projects, individually decorated candles, liturgical drama or dance during the Christmas Morning service, etc. Be sensitive to those church members who are single, or separated from their families. Honorary grandparents, aunts and uncles can be very rewarding people for children to work with — but beware of talking as if all the adults were parents.

* Amid all the bustle, you might find people grateful for a quiet, reflective "Are you ready for Christmas?" session at some point during the last frantic days. Using few, but carefully chosen words, can create a welcome sense of peace and stillness. Lighting candles can be particularly appropriate at this time of year, along with short, appropriate verses of Scripture (e.g. Isaiah 9.2; Isaiah 60.1–2; John 1.5; Revelation 21.24 etc). Incense could also help people by providing a visual focus for their prayers, as they watch the smoke rise up. Even people who would not normally tolerate incense can find this a restful way to pray at times of stress; and it's biblical too (see Psalm 141.1–2 and Revelation 5.8!) All you need is a metal bowl, a charcoal disk and a supply of incense; then invite people to sprinkle a few grains of incense on the charcoal and offer a prayer, aloud or silently, as the smoke rises.

Pentecost is losing its place as an official state holiday, but for Christians of many traditions it remains an important commemoration.

* Will anyone be organizing a big ecumenical Pentecost Praise celebration at an evocative central venue in your area next Pentecost? If so — will your church be going, and how can you make the most of the learning opportunity? If not — why don't you?

* A quiet day or study awayday at Pentecost might be based around the letters to the seven churches in Revelation: how, in our day and our situation, can we "hear what the Spirit is saying to the churches"?

Hallowe'en is a different case altogether. Not many of the Christian churches still make much of the Feast of All Saints; but the pagan Samhain is alive and kicking its way out of the wrappings the early Christian missionaries put round it. Some churches run "Alternative Hallowe'en Parties" for their children and young people, with light–hearted teaching on what Christians believe about life after death and the struggle between good and evil. Possible games might include "Pin the Halo on the Saint" and some lively interactive drama around, say, Revelation 12.7–12 or Matthew 12.22–29. Planning the party, and thinking through what beliefs and understandings lie behind what you are doing, will teach the adults involved a great deal; so may the young people!

Dedication festivals, patronal feasts and chapel anniversaries offer the chance of a seriously light–hearted look at your history as a church.

• What are your roots? How much can you find out about the people who have "been church before you" on your patch? Can you pick up some important moment in your past to celebrate, with things to say about the issues and opportunities you face today? In what ways are you "still the people your forebears were", and in what ways are you different?

Time Capsule

Begin by agreeing your "zero year": the furthest back living memory can take you. There must be at least one person present who can tell you what your church was like in that year, either from first–hand knowledge or from what they remember being told as a child.

Divide into groups of four and five. Give the groups a few minutes to pool everything they know about what the church was like in "zero year" — your own church and the Church in general. Gather the results on a large sheet of paper headed with the year number.

Now jump forward ten years and do it again. Repeat this until you reach the most recent decade year. As you draw nearer to the present, the groups will need more time to pool their memories, and the sheets of paper will get dramatically more crowded. Finally, make one more ten–year leap, into the future, and ask the groups to predict what the church will be like in that year.

Now you've gathered all this information, display it somewhere for other members of the congregation to enjoy. If it has produced gems of community history, could somebody make an artistically lettered version for display in, say, a local public library?

OTHER FESTIVITIES

Family occasions offer plenty of scope for learning activities.

* How does your church *welcome the newly born?* Do you offer new parents any help with thinking out how to bring up their children in faith? Are you good, as a church, at including babies in your worship? Are you good at learning from babies?

* How are young people and new adult Christians prepared for *admission to adult membership?* Working with them as they take stock of what faith means to them can be a powerful learning experience for the educators. Do you spread the benefit of this among a team of lay and ordained people working as colleagues, or leave it all to the clergy?

* What kind of *marriage preparation* do you offer? Is it all concerned with telling the couple about Christian marriage doctrine and where to stand during the service (both of which are important!), or does it also encourage them to explore their expectations about marriage, and strengthen the foundations for good communications between them in married life?

* Do you offer people support in coping with *bereavement?* The loss of someone close is a time of concentrated learning for many people — yet this society often isolates the bereaved, encouraging them to cheer up and stop being morbid, and denying them the opportunity to talk through the deep and painful insights bereavement is bringing them.

* Are your *funerals* times of genuine celebration, grieving joy and hope? This must not be done insensitively, or forced on the mourners by any species of moral blackmail; but the sorrowing joy of Calvary, the bitter wine of hope amid loss, can make a Christian funeral one of the most painfully beautiful of all feasts.

Choosing leaders for preparation courses around personal cusps of
this kind, and for bereavement support, calls for more than usual
care. Listening skills are crucial. People who can only listen for a
sentence or two before they must start talking themselves are
unsuitable for this work, however good the things they say might
be.

Leadership preparation should give the leaders ample chance to
talk through their own experiences around parenthood, or marriage, or bereavement and loss. By dealing with their own baggage
beforehand, they make it easier for themselves to listen carefully
and supportively to the people they will be working with. Only
good listening can help ensure that the teaching they offer will be
useful, and not dismissed as irrelevant or even insulting.

SEASONS OF PREPARATION

Lent is the classic season for adult education to flourish in all its
fullness. Most churches either have Lent groups each year, or
worry that they ought to.

Planning for Lent can usefully begin as early as September
(some churches start at Pentecost!). If your Lent programme repre-
sents your main investment of time, energy and other resources in
organized adult education, it is worth thinking through how best to
use it.

- Is a *national ecumenical course* being prepared, and if so, will
  you be taking part — as your only Lent provision, or as one of
  several options? If you are working ecumenically (increasingly
  many churches now do), which other churches will you seek
  co–operation with? Can you form a joint steering committee to
  manage the planning process? How will the individual churches
  be invited to express their views of what, and how, you should
  study?

- What *topic or topics* will your course or courses cover? Are
  particular teaching needs being expressed among the congregation, which a Lent course could usefully address? Are you
  aware of practical issues coming up in the next year, for which
  a Lent course could be valuable preparation? Have you come
  across any particularly good course materials that you fancy
  using, or adapting to suit your own circumstances? Who chooses

them — you, the education committee, the church council? If it is you, who else should you consult, and how can you best do that? If not, what information will you need to provide the decision–makers with, to help them make an informed decision? How, and when, will you do that?

- What *practical arrangements* need planning? How many study groups will you organize, and where will they meet? Are you a church that prefers to meet in people's homes, on church premises, in the manse or parsonage? Is it better to have all the meetings on the same evening, or to go for a scatter of different days and times of day? Will any of the meetings be associated with acts of worship? Will the preaching at your main Sunday worship be co–ordinated with what the groups are doing? (This could be quite complicated if your preacher is left juggling the demands of the lectionary against three parallel and very different Lent courses!)

- Is this a golden opportunity to *recruit new leaders?* People are often less unwilling to be drawn into leading something which is familiar, like a Lent group, than to leap into the unknown. Here's your chance to finger the people you've had your eye on all year. If they say, "I'd love to but I can't fit it in this year" — note them down for next year!

Leader training for Lent ought to include an opportunity for the leaders to try out together, under somebody else's leadership, a sample of the course material they will be tackling in their groups. New leaders would benefit from some basic guidance about what leadership involves and what their responsibilities are. Who better to give it than the more experienced leaders, who can refresh their own memories in the process. One session together of about two hours in length, with a more general discussion about what leaders do and why, followed by a taste of the coursework, and finishing up with a chance to review the practical arrangements, should be enough for most courses. If you are proposing an unusually ambitious and adventurous choice of learning methods, or if you have a large number of nervous new leaders, it may be best to run a preparatory session ahead of each week's work; but don't forget that this would double the leaders' time commitment, which could create its own problems.

In some churches *Advent,* the traditional preparation season for Christmas, is starting to be taken almost as seriously as Lent.

Advent is a shorter season, and the pressures on people's time may make it difficult for many to fit in an extended course, particularly if their employers are asking them to work longer hours than usual. It is worth thinking about, however, to see if you can find an appropriate pattern for your church.

- Because of the intense secular pressure to do Christmas things during Advent, there are usually plenty of study resources available on radio and television. This might let you try a "dispersed" course, particularly for people who find it difficult to be out and about in winter conditions, where everyone watches/listens in their own home, then Sunday fellowship includes a chance to talk over the week's insights together.

Working up to any major celebration can be a learning opportunity: for example, an approaching church or chapel centenary may inspire all manner of learning activities in the weeks, months or even years leading up to it. The learning possibilities of working down from celebrations afterwards should not be overlooked either.

BIBLE STUDY

Two days later there was a wedding at Cana–in–Galilee. The mother of Jesus was there, and Jesus and his disciples were also among the guests. The wine gave out, so Jesus's mother said to him, "They have no wine left." He answered, "That is no concern of mine. My hour has not yet come." His mother said to the servants, "Do whatever he tells you." There were six stone water–jars standing near, of the kind used for Jewish rites of purification; each held from twenty to thirty gallons. Jesus said to the servants, "Fill the jars with water," and they filled them to the brim. "Now draw some off," he ordered, "and take it to the master of the feast"; and they did so. The master tasted the water now turned into wine, not knowing its source, though the servants who had drawn the water knew. He hailed the bridegroom and said, "Everyone else serves the best wine first, and the poorer only when the guests have drunk freely; but you have kept the best wine till now."

So Jesus performed at Cana–in–Galilee the first of the signs which revealed his glory and led his disciples to believe in him. (John 2.1–11)

1. Read the passage aloud, and do your best to listen with fresh ears, as if you were hearing this story for the first time. Try to forget you already know what happens. Does it say anything particular to you about the way our human celebrations can be transformed if we invite Jesus in?

2. Have you ever been at a celebration where "the wine ran out"? What happened? Did someone save the day? Could you do anything? If you were back there now, what might you try?

3. Choose whichever of the following people you find it easiest to identify with: Jesus' mother; the servants who drew the water; the master of the feast; the other guests; the bridegroom. How do you think they feel about what has just happened? What do you think they would like to say to Jesus now? What would they like to say to each other? (If you are studying the passage with others, you could each choose a different person or group to work on. After allowing yourselves a reasonable time to reflect, compare notes.) Think about the parts the various people play in the story. Can their actions teach you anything useful about organizing celebrations in the Christian family?

4. The Gospel calls this a "sign" which revealed Jesus' glory and led his disciples to believe in him. Do you feel celebrations in your church have the kind of joyfulness that gives a glimpse of the glory of Jesus? Do your special occasions seem to leave people strengthened in faith, as well as giving them a good time? Have you any ideas about how to enhance this?

5. Jesus himself was obviously fond of parties — see, for instance, Mark 21.4–20, Luke 19.1–7. One of his favourite pictures of the Kingdom of God is as a great feast. Will "Any excuse for a party!" do as a motto for a Christian church?

FOR THE LOVE OF LEARNING

Chapter Seven considers learning ventures undertaken simply for the delight of learning. It reviews some possibilities for Bible study groups and for various kinds of courses and events.

If your church is an inspiring place to be, you will probably find all the people some of the time (and some of the people all of the time) becoming fired up with the sheer joy of Christian learning. There is so much pleasure to be had from learning together: "Taste and see that the Lord is good" (Psalm 34.8).

New Christians who come to faith with no real knowledge of Christianity have the excitement of discovering Christian belief as something fresh — all the riches of the Bible and Christian tradition to explore, all the great stories to hear for the first time.

Established Christians have the pleasure of exploring familiar surroundings: they can learn from the Bible and from Christian tradition in depth, already having the basic knowledge to build on. The more study opportunities a person has already enjoyed, the more they have to gain from taking their studies further.

Particular blessings can result if people thoroughly at home with the Bible, and with the practical concerns of Christian faith, have the chance to study with eager new Christians whose insight has the sharpness and freshness only possible when you don't yet know what kind of answers you are looking for.

Unexpected questions, put to people with the knowledge to answer them, can result in floods of new light. "When, therefore, a teacher of the law has become a learner in the kingdom of Heaven, he is like a householder who can produce from his store things new and old." (Matthew 13.51–52)

SHARING TO LEARN

Blessed Lord Jesus,
friend and brother,
may we see you more clearly
love you more dearly
and follow more nearly
day by day.

Every congregation has enormous resources of Christian learning to draw on — far more than it could ever do justice to. The Holy Spirit is constantly at work educating every Christian; tithing the treasures of understanding each one of us has been given would provide more than enough to feed any study group. There are no "ordinary Christians": "...each of us has been given a special gift, a particular share in the bounty of Christ." (Ephesians 4.7)

Not many Christians are in the habit of tithing their knowledge of God. Most have little confidence in the value of their own insights, and see Christian learning as a matter of listening to wiser folk. A few are confident, assured, and offer far more than their fair tithe. We need to develop a Magnificat faith, worthy of the God who "hath put down the mighty from their seats: and hath exalted the humble and meek".

For that to happen, shy Christians have to find the courage and trust to offer their full tithe of insights for sharing. Fluent, high-powered Christians have to find the grace and humility to hold back, and offer no more than their tithe. All of us have to learn how to choose out from all our experiences the tithe that will be most rewarding for others to receive.

To become a faith-sharing church means unlearning the worldly wisdom that says some people are worth listening to, and others aren't. This can only be done through careful and rigorously honest discernment. Building people's confidence calls for accurate praise that they can recognize as valid. Many adult Christians don't give themselves credit for the expertise they have — but they won't learn to, unless the encouragement they are given rings true

---

Timeshares

This is the simplest form of faith-sharing exercise. Each group member in turn is asked to offer a contribution, without interruption or discussion. Plenty of silence between speakers helps everyone take in what is being shared.

Members might be asked to:

- Talk about a place that helps them to understand God — or a person who shows something of God to them — or a time in their life that brought them closer to God — or a smell that particularly takes their mind to God.

- Bring a "thing" (it might be a piece of jewellery, or house-hold object, or ornament, or even an item of rubbish) that tells them something important about God, and while passing it round for the other members to handle, explain why they have brought it.

- Bring, or describe, a picture that shows something of what God means to them — or play, and talk about, a piece of music that turns them to God — or read aloud a poem, or passage from a book.

Timeshares work well with groups that haven't tried anything like this before.

They are also valuable on the end of a long day when people have had enough of discussing. They make a good first–evening activity for residential weekends; although people may be tired from travelling, the quality of reflection that a good timeshare offers can work on people overnight to produce exciting results the next morning.

Sharing Faith with New Christians

Faith–sharing groups are a useful way to involve lay people with goodwill but no special educational expertise in educating new believers. Anyone willing to try putting their own faith into words has a valuable part to play. Quiet people who don't find words easily can be a big help to anxious newcomers. It is very reassuring to see that being a Christian doesn't necessarily mean pouring out floods of wonderful wisdom at the drop of a hat; and people of few words are frequently well worth listening to when they do find something they want to say.

A faith–sharing group needs to be small enough for everyone to have a fair chance of joining in the conversation: between six and ten people is about right, with a mixture of new and more experienced Christians. It is very important to give newcomers time to tell their own stories. Faith–sharing is a bit like a maternity clinic: you listen fascinated to the accounts of other people's labour and delivery, and descriptions of their babies, because you know that presently you can tell them about your own experiences and your own even more beautiful baby. In a good faith–sharing group, everyone is given a respectful hearing, because each person's path into faith is different and important.

Programme for a five week course:

Week One: How did I first find faith in God?
Week Two: What does Jesus mean to me?
Week Three: What do I believe God wants for his world?
Week Four: What am I finding easiest about being a Christian, at the moment? What am I finding hardest?
Week Five: What do I need now to help me go further into faith? What do I want to do for myself? What do I want to do with other people? What resources do I need? What practical next steps shall I take?

Basic outline for each session:

• Begin with a time for building up fellowship with one another. In the first week, ask each person to say a little about who they are and where they come from. In the rest of the sessions, ask each person in turn to share one good thing that has happened to them since the group last met.

• Ask each person to say what they want to about the week's theme. Timid people may need a little gentle prompting, but there should be no discussion of what is offered until everyone has had their chance to speak.

• Encourage everyone to join in drawing out the connections between what different people have said, and adding whatever else they feel prompted to share.

• Move into a time of free prayer, offering to God all that you have discovered together.

• End with a simple shared act of worship — maybe lighting a candle, reading a Bible passage aloud, singing a hymn or song that everyone knows. Suitable Bible passages might be: week one, Jeremiah 1.4–8; week two, John 4.7–14; week three, Isaiah 35; week four, 2 Corinthians 4.5–16; week five, Hebrews 11.8–16.

Leadership in Faith–sharing Groups

Some groups work well without an official leader: all the members share responsibility for arranging the meetings and making sure that they run in a satisfying way. Others prefer to give the task of leading the discussion to one member.

In a successful group, every member's contribution is treated as equally important. This is not at all the same thing as everybody speaking for exactly the same time as everybody else. It is vital to respect people's individuality, and let them make their contribution to the group in a way that feels right to them.

Prokrustes, the mythical Greek robber, had a bed that he forced travellers to lie on. If they took up more space than he thought they should, he cut them off at the knees. If they didn't take up enough space to satisfy him, he hit them with a big stick until they spread out a bit. Prokrustes had altogether the wrong idea about sensitive group leadership.

Encouraging *people who don't contribute to discussion* needs a delicate touch. Shy people hate to be made conspicuous. If someone has sat in silence for the first half hour of a discussion, a hearty "So what do *you* think about all this, Carmen?" is hardly ever the best way forward.

- *Watch carefully* for any indication that the quiet person wants to speak – sitting forward, licking his/her lips, trying to catch your eye. A group can easily squash a quiet person's attempt to join in, without meaning to; it only needs somebody else to speak at the same moment.

- *Pay close attention yourself* to what the quiet person says, and if you get the chance, bring the group back to it later: "Does that link up with what Jim was saying?"

- *Leave spaces in the discussion* for people to reflect on what has been said, and think about any comments they might like to make. Some people need time to put what they want to say into words.

- *Have a quiet word after the session* to find out why the person wasn't speaking. Be sensitive about this, or you could make an already self–conscious person even more so. There may be a personal reason they didn't want to mention in front of the group. On the other hand, some people are genuinely content to sit and listen for almost the whole time, and prefer only to speak when they have a distinctive point to make. That is a perfectly valid way to join in a group discussion. Beware of making people feel it is wrong to be quiet.

Enabling *people who talk too much* to take a more constructive role needs other tactics.

- *Structure the discussion* so that, for example, at regular intervals every member in turn is asked whether they have any comment they want to make at that point ("no" is a permissible answer). Be friendly but firm with people who want to comment on everyone else's comment.

- *Invite somebody else to speak* before the talker can leap in.

- In a tactful way, *point out* that the group has already gained some good insights from the talker, but hasn't yet heard what other people think.

- If the person realizes they have a problem, develop a secret *signal* between the two of you for use when they are talking too much: a raised eyebrow, a pull on your left earlobe, a wiggle of your fingers? If you have the same problem yourself (some of us do!), the arrangement could be mutal.

- If all else fails, *ask the talker to act as group scribe,* and when they interrupt another speaker, say "Have you got Mary's point down yet, Fred?"

BIBLE STUDY

Bible study is the basic requirement of adult Christian learning.

Many adult Christians use daily Bible reading notes.

- Does your church *recommend a particular scheme* to members? If so, who makes sure new members are introduced to it, and what guidance are people given on how to make best use of it? How are the themes and concerns of the scheme picked up in wider church life, to enhance everyone's sense of "learning together separately"?

- Do you ever offer *group study sessions* to help people take stock of what they are discovering through private study? These could be occasional or regular, depending on demand.

- Are *linked Bible study suggestions* provided as part of your major educational ventures, to give people a programme of home Bible study alongside, say, a Lent group series or leadership training course?

- Could Bible Society's *Know the Scriptures Bible Reading Certificate* offer a useful structure for introducing new Christians (and interested others) to a more detailed knowledge of the Bible? It provides a programme for reading through the books of the New Testament, with an introduction to each section of reading, and test questions to sum up the learning from each unit. Answers are sent to Bible Society for marking, and a certificate is issued on completion of the course. The course pack also includes a cassette tape of background information, and suggestions are offered for small group tutorials to accompany the private course of study.

Bible Study Groups

Studying the Bible in a group opens up much richer possibilities than solitary study. Everyone you will ever meet in the rest of your life has something unique to teach you about understanding the Bible. It is often the people who are most timid and hard to draw out, who have the most valuable insights to share. Difficult people, whose views you don't agree with, can lead you to truths you would never have seen without their interference.

Bible Society produces a wide range of resources for group Bible study — see the latest catalogue for details. These include guides to particular books of the Bible, study courses arranged round discipleship themes and issues, and material particularly suited to specific age or interest groups.

Simple group study exercises:

- *"Bring & Bible"* studies. Every member is asked to bring a favourite Bible passage on a given theme. Each person in turn reads their passage aloud and says a word or two about why they chose it. Everyone is then invited to say what thoughts and feelings have been conjured up for them. Have their own understandings been changed by what other people have said?

- *Bible Drama.* An event from Scripture, or a passage of Scripture teaching, is presented to the group and explored through improvised drama. *The Dramatised Bible*/ offers simple dramatized readings for most biblical narratives. The group could produce its own straight dramatization of the chosen text.

You might opt for working with a more adventurous kind of script, either taken from the many excellent published collections available or written by one of the group. Some of the most rewarding studies come from simply giving the group's creative impulses free rein. There is no need for the results to be "performed" to anyone; the learning comes from the exploration.

- *Bible Sharing.* The whole group listens as the passage chosen for study is read aloud. After a time of silence for reflection, each person repeats aloud the words or phrases that particularly caught their attention. The passage is read aloud a second time. Everyone is then invited to share whatever insights have been sparked off for them. The discussion often leads naturally into free prayer and intercession. At the end of the study time the text is read aloud one last time, to bring the discussion firmly back to the word of Scripture.

Linking group studies of this kind to (one or more of) the following Sunday's set readings enriches the participants' sharing in worship as well as their sense of being grounded in the Bible.

Bible study groups can meet anywhere: in a church hall, a member's home, a garden (weather permitting!), even, for agile groups, on top of a mountain. It is worth thinking about the possibilities of unusual venues. For example, if you are planning as a church to go on a pilgrimage to somewhere interesting, could that offer you the chance of, perhaps:

- studying the persecution experiences of the early Church (such as Acts 12.1–19) in a dank and atmospheric crypt?

- studying Isaiah's vision in the Temple (Isaiah 6.1–10) in one of the great holy buildings of our own day?

- studying a lakeside Gospel passage (such as Matthew 14.13–34) by the side of a genuine lake?

If your church, or some members of it, should have the opportunity of visiting the Holy Land together, that gives enormous scope for imaginative Bible study before, during and after the visit. Understanding the geography of Bible events from the inside, by yourself climbing around on the landscape Jesus knew, can open astonishing new veins of understanding, to be quarried afterwards at leisure.

The harrowing political situation in the Holy Land at the present day helps to guard us against prettifying the life of Jesus. He lived all his life, as texts like Matthew 2.16–18, Luke 13.1–3 and Mark 15.7 make clear, in a time of political unrest and violence that had many similarities to the present. Grasping this truth can help us to see more clearly the kind of pressures that Caiaphas, Pilate, the Sadducees and Pharisees, the Zealots and the ordinary citizens faced when they had to decide how to respond to Jesus.

Modern Biblical Criticism

Many adult Christians today find it difficult to know how they should see the truth of Scripture. Did Balaam's donkey genuinely talk (Numbers 22.28) and the sun stand still at Gibeon (Joshua 10.13) — and what do we make of the Gospel miracles? Do Matthew 26.6–13, Mark 14.3–9, Luke 7.36–50 and John 12.1–8 all describe the same incident, and if so, can we ever really know just what happened? All four Evangelists describe the arrest, trial and execution of Jesus, but the descriptions are so different in detail that it becomes almost impossible to see any of them as an exact historical statement by today's standards. Comparing Acts 15.1–2 with Galatians 2.11–14 suggests that either Paul or the writer of Acts has taken liberties with the facts of Peter's role in what must have been a very fraught situation.

An adult faith needs to be able to tussle with these kinds of problem, in knowing how to rely on the Bible for truth and guidance. It isn't a unique or even a particularly unusual difficulty. Any reader of newspapers knows that you have to make allowances for the writer's style and the editorial policy if you want to guess at the facts behind the headlines. However, many adult Christians feel uneasy at the idea of examining the Bible text critically — that using your trained judgement to tell what the writer is doing and why, is somehow disrespectful to the word of God.

If you want the adult members of your church to be able to think seriously about what the Bible has to teach them, they need to be comfortable with Bible truth. They can't keep their faith and their intelligence in separate pockets. People who are encouraged to find ways of understanding the Bible that make real sense to them, are likely to be much happier and more confident when it comes to sharing their faith with non–believers.

Modern biblical criticism offers tools for opening up the truth of Scripture, by looking at the structure of the text, the ways in which important words are used, the ways the different writers put their ideas together. Biblical scholars are a very mixed bag, and frequently disagree with one another's findings. The world of critical scholarship is a confusing and discouraging one for many adult Christians, who wish they could tell just exactly what they *are* being asked to believe.

In some churches, clergy and theologically trained lay educators have offered courses which set out the basic principles of modern critical scholarship, and show people how to use these principles in their own private study. There are good modern commentaries, available in a range of theological flavours, which explain the more widely accepted findings in a straightforward and accessible form. If your church wants to encourage people in learning to appreciate critical scholarship, it's worth building up a church library with a range of styles and approaches, so that people can browse until they find something that speaks to them.

Another way of approaching the issues is to set up opportunities for people to discuss together what they mean by "the truth of Scripture". How do they use the Bible, and what kind of truth do they think it holds? It is sometimes easier for lay people to start by discussing this in the absence of their clergy, and then perhaps on a later occasion bring in an ordained minister or lay theologian to help the group go further into the questions being raised.

LEARNING FROM EXPERTS AND ENTHUSIASTS

This can be great fun and very rewarding. Besides calling on the expertise in your education team:

- Build up a good *intelligence system* outside your borders to spot other clergy and lay people with educational skills. It helps if your team is known to be positive about invitations from others.

- Are there *universities or colleges* in your area with theology departments, or training institutions for ordinands? If so, staff members might respond positively to invitations, particularly if you are only asking them for a once-off or short, well-defined time commitment. Alternatively, try asking an academic theologian to spend an evening with your education team, then take it from there yourselves.

- Does your *denomination* provide outside expertise? Is there a list somewhere of tutors who train lay preachers, and could that be a useful source of contacts? Is there an ecumenical educators' grapevine you could tap into?

- Do you have a *talent spotting system* in your own congregation? You may find people are reluctant to serve as "experts" in front of their fellow church members, or fall victim to the Nazareth effect – "A prophet never lacks honour except in his home town, among his relations and his own family" (Mark 6.4). Nevertheless, it is worth keeping track of the resources you have in your midst. Pairing up someone knowledgeable about a subject with one of your education team to act as "ringmaster" can spark off lively and rewarding learning occasions.

A useful model for course leadership was developed by Beatrice Shearer for the Step By Step project in east London. The course content comes as modules of three sessions each — "Using the Bible", "Knowing God and the Difference It Makes", "Listening and Helping"; choose whatever areas of knowledge and practice are most worthwhile in your situation. An opening introductory module helps people get to know each other and think about what they will be doing. A final module helps them take stock of all they have learned together, and think about what happens next. A group pastor, who works with the group throughout, takes responsibility for the members' pastoral needs, such as support and encouragement. Different tutors are recruited for each module; they come in, do their three weeks and go away again, with advice from the group pastor to help maintain continuity and avoid duplication of subject matter. This has the great advantage of limiting the amount of time each tutor is asked for to an easily manageable level. Choosing the right person for group pastor is crucial for a successful course: lay preachers and readers, having themselves been through extended training, can be very good in this role.

DESIGNING LEARNING EVENTS

You may sometimes have the chance to organize a large–scale learning event, perhaps working with other churches in your neighbourhood or region. You could even aim to draw in non–churchgoers. That would mean:

- choosing a theme that would interest other people in your local community as well as the active Christians;

- finding a venue that non–churchgoers would be comfortable with; perhaps a community centre or school hall rather than a church–owned building;

- advertising the event widely, not just on church noticeboards, and designing the publicity with as broad an appeal as possible;

- thinking out ways to make the atmosphere friendly, welcoming and open;

- designing the event so that non Christians could take part in all the activities as equals, not outsiders.

The learning cycle Do–Look–Think–Plan is a good guide for designing adult learning events. Different people like to come in at different points in the cycle. Activist types want to be up and doing straight away. More reflective people prefer to start by watching and listening. Theorists are eager to see the subject as a whole, and draw out connections with other areas of Christian faith and practice. Pragmatical characters are most interested in how what they are learning can be used back home, and how well it will work. This just goes to show that you can't please all of the people all of the time — but a good event design needs to have something in it for everyone.

The possibilities for good learning activities are endless. They may involve many people or few; they may break new ground, or discover new depths in what is well–loved and familiar; they may last for years, or be over in ten minutes. The point is this: "that out of the treasures of his glory he may grant you inward strength and power through his Spirit, that through faith Christ may dwell in your hearts in love. With deep roots and firm foundations may you, in company with all God's people, be strong to grasp what is the breadth and length and height and depth of Christ's love, and to know it, though it is beyond knowledge. So may you be filled with the very fullness of God." (Ephesians 3.16–19)

LEARNING CYCLE

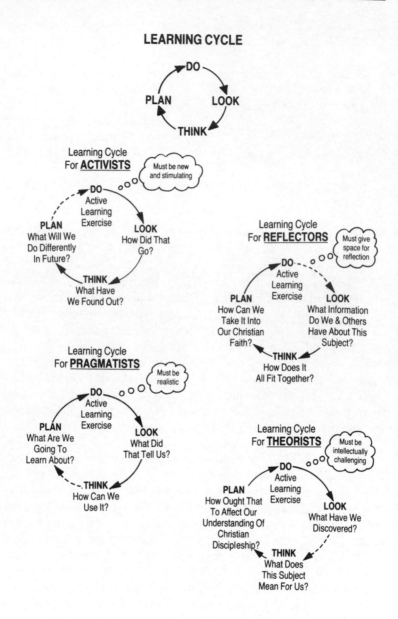

For more details of the learning styles theory on which this model is
based, see The Manual of Learning Styles *and* Using your Learning Styles
*both by Peter Honey and Alan Mumford; available from Peter Honey,
Ardingly House, 10 Linden Avenue, Maidenhead, Berkshire, SL6 6HB.*

BIBLE STUDY

LORD, your unfailing love reaches to the heavens,
your faithfulness to the skies.
Your righteousness is like the lofty mountains,
your justice like the great deep;
LORD who saves man and beast,
how precious is your unfailing love!
Gods and frail mortals seek refuge in the shadow of your
   wings.
They are filled with the rich plenty of your house,
and you give them to drink from the stream of your delights;
for with you is the fountain of life,
and by your light we are enlightened. (Psalm 36.5–9)

1. Read the passage aloud, and listen to the flow of it. Think back
   over your own life as a Christian. What things have most "filled
   you with the rich plenty of God's house"? Where have you
   found "the fountain of life"? Are there other images in the
   psalm that particularly speak to you? What do they summon
   up? If you are working in a group, take five or ten minutes to
   reflect in silence before you start to compare notes on what has
   particularly struck you.

2. What have been the most valuable learning experiences your
   church has shared over the last couple of years? Try to make a
   complete list, either writing them down or drawing symbols to
   represent them. Sketch in the way the different experiences
   relate to each other — did one lead to another? Did they have
   important features in common? Were the same people involved,
   as leaders or participants? What do you feel have been the main
   gains from these experiences?

3. *"Your righteousness is like the lofty mountains,*
   your justice like the great deep..."

   How much enthusiasm do you find people in your church have
   for tackling justice issues together? What has been tried in the
   last twelve months, and how did it go? Was there anything that
   particularly delighted, surprised, or shocked you? How well do
   you feel the balance has been kept between studying God's
   unfailing love and faithfulness on the one hand, and looking
   into the demands of righteousness and justice on the other?

4. *"They are filled with the rich plenty of your house,*
   and you give them to drink from the stream of your delights..."

Draw a garden to represent your church's current learning activities. Do you find yourself wanting to draw a single open space, or a number of different kinds of garden area linked together? Put in:

- *trees* — long–term established learning habits;
- *flowers* — learning activities blossoming at present;
- *green shoots* — exciting possibilities;
- a large *compost heap* for all the finished blooms, unnoticed opportunities, casual low–key learning and other miscellaneous bits and pieces that go to enrich the soil.

What kinds of gardening are you doing? What effects do your activities, as an educator, or team of educators, seem to be having on the garden? What has gone into the compost heap for your whole church, over the last twelve months? Any seeds that you hope might sprout in future? Any weed seeds that you would definitely *not* want to see sprouting?

5. What would be your personal dream learning opportunity? Imagine you could have unlimited time and money to spend on something educational (in the broadest possible interpretation of the word). What would you choose, and why? What group of people would you organize it for? Where would you go? What would you do?

Notes

1. Compiler Michael Perry, published by Bible Society/Marshall Pickering, ISBN 0–564–05135–7.